ACTIVISM THAT MAKES SENSE

ACTIVISM
THAT MAKES SENSE

CONGREGATIONS AND COMMUNITY
ORGANIZATION

Gregory F. Augustine Pierce

ACTA Publications

Chicago, Illinois

The Publisher gratefully acknowledges the use of the following materials:

The selection from *Bread and Wine* by Ignazio Silone (copyright Darina Silone) is used with permission of his wife.

The selection from *One Flew Over the Cuckoo's Nest* by Ken Kesey (copyright 1982 by Ken Kesey) is reprinted with permission of Viking Penguin, Inc.

The summary of "Father Hit Cult Where It Hurts—Pocketbook" by Anne Keegan (copyright 1982 by *Chicago Tribune*) is used with permission of Chicago Tribune.

"Eliciting a Community's Story: The Parish Interview Process" by William Droel (from *Service* #3, July/August/September 1982, Volume 9) is used with permission of Paulist Press.

"The Biblical Imperative" (1981) is used with permission of the Queens Citizens Organization.

Selections by Andrew Greeley and Nicholas Von Hoffman are used with permission of the authors.

All biblical quotes are from the *New Jerusalem Bible* unless otherwise noted. All definitions are from *Webster's New Twentieth Century Dictionary* (Second Edition).

Library of Congress Catalog Card Number: 83-82016

ISBN: 0-914070-53-3

Published by   ACTA Publications
                4848 N. Clark Street
                Chicago, Illinois 60640
                312-271-1030

Printed and bound in the United States of America

CONTENTS

v

7. LEADERS:
ARE THERE ANY VOLUNTEERS?

CONCLUSION: UNCOMFORTABLE NECESSITY

APPENDICES

To Mom and Dad

He's that first-born son
He's that son-of-a-gun
He don't like to walk
He just likes to run

First Born
Kate and Anna McGarrigle

PREFACE

It has been almost ten years since I wrote this book. Many things have changed in my life and in the world in that time, but one thing that has remained constant is my belief in the value for congregations to become involved in community organization.

There are many reasons for congregations not to join a community organization. It costs money, it takes time, it insures conflict—both inside and outside the congregation. Then there are those infuriating, agitating organizers!

Yet community organizations have proven their value to congregations over and over again. They remain one of the few viable ways to produce real, measurable victories on a whole range of issues of vital concern to a congregation: city services, housing, crime, transportation, schools, etc. Issues such as these determine the viability of the communities in which the congregation functions and therefore the future of the congregation itself.

Major sources of contemporary family problems are the economic, cultural and neighborhood pressures in our society. Congregations often end up merely dealing with the effects of these problems on their members. A strong, broad-based community organization, however, can offer congregations a way of dealing with these pressures at their root cause by helping the congregation learn how to negotiate with those institutions of society which are undermining family values.

Every congregation needs a strategy for the identification, recruitment and training of new leaders for the congregation. Most do not have one. Many congregations rely on the surest recipe for failure in leadership development: asking for volunteers and accepting what comes forward. A good community organization develops new, trained leaders for the congregation as part of its overall effort.

Community organization also offers congregations a different way of getting people together across racial, ethnic, religious and economic boundaries. If the organization is open and broad-based enough, it will include a great variety of people. They will come together not out of a desire to engage in some sort of sensitivity exercise but out of mutual self-interest.

Finally, by providing the opportunity for theological reflection on the connection between religion and the world, community organization offers to any congregation perhaps its most important service. Community organization provides the grist for a congregation's reflection on its role in the world. Good theological reflection is based on experience, and the best theological reflection is based on experience obtained communally.

I thank once again all the leaders and organizers in congregations and community organizations throughout the country who have enriched my life. I encourage them to continue their good work in making this world a slightly better place.

Gregory F. Augustine Pierce
Chicago, 1991

FOREWORD

George Orwell's *1984* is a novel about "non-persons" in a totalitarian society. With our own mass culture and pervasive government and multinational corporations on one hand, and with us—isolated, ragged individuals—on the other, some posit that we are not far from *1984*.

The concept of mediating structures is now gaining wide currency in social science circles as our best defense against such totalitarianism. In their seminal book *To Empower People: The Role of Mediating Structures in Public Policy*, Peter Berger and Richard Neuhaus define mediating structures as "those institutions standing between the individual in his private life and the large institutions of public life."[1] As examples of such institutions they name the family, the neighborhood, the congregation, and the voluntary association. The present danger is that cultural strains and individual expectations are so high in contemporary American society that these deteriorating mediating structures will no longer be able to shelter us in this alienating world.

Gregory Pierce's book is about this crisis. His theme is the necessity for the local religious congregation to accept its role as a mediating institution. He offers a vehicle for accomplishing that goal which has an honored history in this country: community organization.

Pierce's brand of community organization can trace its heritage to 1941 when Saul Alinsky started the Back of the Yards Neighborhood Council in my Southwest Side neighborhood of Chicago. Some writers have debated the "Alinsky method" and more recently some have written "how-to" manuals based on Alinsky practice. This work, however, is the first systematic rationale for the involvement of local congregations in this type of activism.

There has always been a connection between community organization and theological reflection. Community organization owes a theoretical debt to Protestantism's social gospel, Catholicism's personalism, and the Jewish commitment to justice for the oppressed.

In practice, this connection has not always been noticeable. Although traveling on very close roads, the local congregation and the community organization have not always fully appreciated how mutually beneficial they are to one another. At times certain organizers have let their personal impatience with organized religion blind them to legitimate concerns of the congregations. Congregations have often responded to organizers with caution and failed to see the value of such men and women to their own mission. As both an active Christian layman and a trained professional organizer, Pierce is able to merge these two roads.

Activism That Makes Sense comes at an opportune time for our nation's domestic consideration. So many people have now fallen through the Republicans' safety net that the need for new ways of protecting the powerless is apparent. The Democrats have proposed few alternatives other than some form of return to their War on Poverty—a conflict which poverty won.

Rather than accepting another layer of bureaucracy in the neighborhoods or welcoming the tired rhetoric of private initiative that is really a Trojan horse for helping the wealthy, we would do well to explore the role of mediating structures for the 1980's and 1990's.

This is also a critical time in our religious thinking. Many people of all faiths are trying to ground their spirituality in justice. They seem most attracted by the lofty causes of world hunger, nuclear disarmament and third world development. There is a question, however, of scale of effectiveness. Some problems command the attention of denominational leaders and national religious bodies. Other concerns are much more successfully dealt with on a local, congregational level. There is a definite link between the two, of course, but sometimes activity is mistaken for effective action.

The major reason why people in the pews don't respond to teaching on justice and peace is that they don't perceive how that teaching affects them. Social justice is hard work. It is not merely a matter of being aware of events in our world. It is taking a hand in shaping those events.

Ultimately, the institutionalization of justice and peace for people in our congregations means holding accountable such mundane things as banks, insurance companies, zoning boards, public utility commissions and courts of law. Gregory Pierce has been quite willing to crawl around inside such institutions for many years. He is a wonderful storyteller and offers clearly focused argumentation. His analysis is witty but thorough, blunt but gentle.

Activism That Makes Sense is based on faith in the perfectibility of our democratic institutions, faith that the reign of God has begun, and faith in the common person. It is a substantial contribution to the theology of lived hope.

William M. Droel

INTRODUCTION:
THE HALLIHANS' BOILER

The boiler was eight years into a ten year warranty when it blew. It was the middle of a cold February with the wind whipping off Jamaica Bay in Queens.

When the man from the Brooklyn Union Gas Company arrived, he quickly determined that the boiler had burst because another part—also installed by them but no longer under warranty—had failed first. It was not, he informed the family, the company's responsibility.

Within fifteen minutes of the repairman's departure, an unsummoned salesman from the Brooklyn Union Gas Company was at the door offering to have a new boiler installed the next day with "convenient" payment plans.

Many families at this point would have signed the contract, hunkered down and added the payments to their already overspent budget. The Hallihans, however, just could not afford $2,500 for a new boiler. They had five children. He worked as the custodian for a nearby church and as a part-time attendant in a gas station. She was a full-time mother. Like most Americans, they were trying to make ends meet.

Because Brendan Hallihan was a janitor, he was able to jimmy the boiler and get the heat in the house up to fifty degrees—enough to keep the pipes from freezing but not enough to allow the family to live in their home. He was able to determine which parts needed to be replaced and called the gas company to order them. After considerable delay, word

4

came that the parts were no longer carried in stock and had to be ordered from Pennsylvania where the boiler had been made. It would take several days.

The cold spell continued, but the Hallihans were frugal enough and angry enough to order the parts. One day later, the company informed them that Pennsylvania was out of the parts and that new parts would have to be recast. It would take another six weeks. The boiler could not be repaired until after Easter.

At this point the Hallihans gave in. They could not go through an entire winter without a boiler. They would have to order the new one and figure out how to pay for it later.

If this story sounds familiar it is because it is repeated so often in the daily experience of most families. The frustration, the injustice, the powerlessness have come to be expected and accepted.

To whom can the family turn for help? One obvious possibility is its church or synagogue. Most local congregations faced with a similar situation—which they are frequently—respond in much the same ways: sympathy, prayers, offers of food and shelter, possibly even a donation toward a new boiler. Seldom do they address the source of the problem—people's inability to deal with large, impersonal institutions like the gas company.

The Hallihans belonged to Our Lady of Grace Catholic Church in the Howard Beach section of New York City. The parish had recently joined the Queens Citizens Organization— a community organization made up of local congregations and civic groups—organized with help from the Industrial Areas Foundation.

I was the organizer for this project at that time, and I was called in by the pastor and lay leaders to discuss the Hallihans' situation. I recommended that they take this issue on at the cause—the policies and practices of the Brooklyn Union Gas Company—and they agreed to try.

We demanded an immediate meeting with officials of the company. They agreed not because of the legitimacy of the

Hallihans' complaint nor as a result of the intervention of the congregation, but because of the reputation of the Queens Citizens Organization for causing trouble.

The night before the hastily arranged meeting, my job as the professional organizer was to quickly teach the inexperienced people of the parish how to negotiate. Our strategy was simple. We prepared an hour-by-hour written reconstruction of the events and demanded a new boiler installed for the Hallihans immediately and at no charge. If we did not get what we wanted, we threatened to go to the media and to the Public Utilities Commission for an investigation—not only of this incident but of the entire sales and service practices of the corporation.

The officials of the gas company took one look at the delegation of twenty-five angry parishioners accompanied by their pastor, the documented research, the picture of the five freezing Hallihan children . . . and the threat. They left the room for a few minutes and returned to offer a new boiler with a five year warranty for the price of the parts they could not produce—about $300.

Our delegation caucused, agreed it was a fair compromise and a victory, and accepted the offer. The next day the Hallihans had their new boiler, without the new monthly payments they had feared.

This episode is an epiphany of the possibilities and the problems—the opportunities and the threats—that involvement in community organization offers to local religious congregations.

I want to analyze this involvement as both a professional organizer and a committed layperson. My examples will be necessarily out of my own experience, but the conclusions will hopefully have some application to all congregations searching for an activism that makes sense.

Chapter 1

ACTIVISM: NOT WHETHER . . . BUT HOW

Fill the earth and conquer it.
Genesis 1:28

Most congregations—Protestant, Catholic or Jewish—would not have acted to solve the Hallihans' boiler problem because it would never have occurred to them to try.

This blind spot is curious. Other voluntary associations—neighborhood councils, political clubs, unions, civil rights organizations, chambers of commerce, fraternal organizations, service groups—would at least consider the possibility of mounting some sort of protest to help their members deal with an injustice.

Yet most people's religious association would not, even though for many Americans their church or synagogue is the primary if not the only organization to which they belong and donate time and money. Faced with a real crisis in one of its families, most congregations stand immobile—despite their almost universal theoretical commitment to social justice.

Often the reason lies in the congregation's theological assumptions. The Judaeo-Christian tradition as filtered through Western philosophy has always had a tension at its core between body and soul, this world and the next, the transcendental and the incarnate.

It is not the purpose of this book to reargue this ancient debate. Until a congregation becomes convinced theologically through study and prayer that the God who acts in history does so through the actions of men and women, it will never act in defense of its values but will rather encourage its members to accept the world the way it is.

For an increasing number of congregations of all persuasions, however, there is no dichotomy between the spiritual and the physical salvation of the world. Social teachings by the leaders of all the major religions, mass communications that bring worldwide injustice to the attention of all, and an increasing sense of the powerlessness of the individual in the face of technological complexity and concentration of wealth have made the concept of activism not only acceptable but necessary to many.

They would agree with formulations such as this one by Sister Mary John Manazan: "The current understanding of salvation sees salvation as the liberation of the whole human being . . . liberation not only from sin, death and hell, but from everything that dehumanizes him (and her) including oppression, exploitation, injustice and dehumanizing poverty."[2]

Many clergy and laity have accepted—intellectually, emotionally and spiritually—the need for active involvement in the problems of the world in order to fulfill the basic religious mission.

They just don't know how to do it successfully.

This book is aimed at them. It suggests community organization as one strategy for activism that can be true to a congregation's values, appropriate to the American experience, and pragmatic in both approach and expectation of success.

As congregations attempt to develop a program of involvement in the affairs of the world, they often find themselves caught in one of several activist traps.

SOCIAL SERVICE

This is the easiest, most obvious, most accepted and most traditional approach to activism. If things are wrong, if people are hurting, then the congregation helps them directly. It is the Sermon on the Mount, the law and the prophets. No one can object, and the congregation feels good that it is doing something to relieve suffering. Many congregations in the United States are now providing this kind of service to one degree or another. Some efforts are quite elaborate, professional and costly: day care centers, counseling, housing for the poor and the elderly. Others are simple and basic: food pantries, clothing drives.

There is one problem with this activity, however. It doesn't work.

It doesn't work in the sense that it never ends, never makes a dent in the problem, is never enough, doesn't change what is causing the problems. It doesn't work in the sense that it wouldn't have helped the Hallihans with their boiler.

Theologian Walter Rauschenbusch explained the frustration many religious people feel in his book *Righteousness of the Kingdom:*

> Why should Christian men wear out their strength in curing the effects of evil and have no word about the evil itself?
>
> Society dumps its moral offal of pauperism and crime upon the church and says: "Here, take these and care for them." And the church works and moans about the unceasing flood of evil and the hopelessness of the task. . . .
>
> The apostolic Church founded the order of deacons to avoid social inequality and to make sure that all want was relieved. Our deacons are still caring for the poor, but after they have become poor. Would it not be entirely in keeping with the spirit of Christ, if some of the nineteenth-century deacons would take it

in hand to care for the poor before they have been made poor, by stopping the causes that pauperize society? Why should the Church of Christ drive a one-horse cart, while the church of Mammon runs an express-train with all modern improvements?[3]

President Ronald Reagan and New York Mayor Edward Koch graphically demonstrated the limits of the social service approach to activism by congregations.

Reagan suggested that if every religious institution in the country "adopted" ten families, it would eliminate the welfare system.

Koch asked each church and synagogue in the city to bed ten homeless men every night in its facility—presumably forever.

The Episcopal bishop of New York, the Rev. Paul Moore, Jr., pointed out the fallacy of these requests in an article entitled "Koch, Reagan, and The Poor": "These remarks are dangerous because they avoid a primary responsibility of government—and push it off on the guilty conscience of well-meaning citizens who, if they took the suggestion seriously, might do untold harm to the recipients and in the process might cripple their parish churches."[4]

On the face of it, Reagan's and Koch's proposals appear to be a case of simple charity. Yet though they are a logical extension of the social service approach that so many congregations have adopted, such plans make no sense precisely because they are so overwhelming, so never-ending, so impossible.

No one would denigrate the good will such direct service programs entail or the real comfort they provide, but it can be said that congregations that adopt exclusively this mode of activism have doomed themselves to a constant attempt to bandage hurts that will never be cured.

INDIVIDUAL ACTIVISM

Faced with the undeniable limitations of the social service approach, many congregations then advocate that their members become individually involved in political activism—of both electoral and non-electoral varieties. The job of the congregation in this model becomes to inform the consciences of the individual member who is then expected to go into the political arena to solve the root causes of the suffering that the social service approach cannot. No judgment is made on those members of the congregation who do not so act, nor is the congregation itself expected to act as a body.

This approach at least recognizes the need for political and radical (in the Latin sense of dealing with the "root causes" of problems) activism. However, it tends to rouse people to individual effort without providing the equipment or the collective backing that would allow them to succeed.

How many members of religious congregations of all faiths have heard exhortations such as these drummed into their heads from the time they were born into or joined their congregation?

Rabbi Morris Adler in *Great Jewish Ideas:*

It becomes the responsibility of each alert and high-minded individual to resist the encroachments upon justice, truth and peace which constitute the foundations of freedom. No man may stand aside and remain neutral in the ongoing struggle to achieve in human life a fuller approximation of virtue and righteousness. To abdicate such an obligation is to abet the forces of evil and to become an accomplice in the perpetuation of wrong.[5]

Peter Berger in *The Noise of the Solemn Assemblies:*

. . . we have stressed the importance for Christians of lucid, fearless perception of social reality. We would go further now and stress not only independence of

thinking but also rebelliousness of attitude. Our time
has had its share of organization men. Now it needs
insurrectionary spirits, adventurers, rebels. And it
needs—very badly indeed—Christian rebels.[6]

Pope Paul VI in *Octogesima Adveniens:*

Let each one examine himself, to see what he has
done up to now, then what he ought to do. It is not
enough to recall principles, state intentions, point to
crying injustices and utter prophetic denunciations;
these words will lack real weight unless they are accompanied for each individual by a livelier awareness
of personal responsibility and by effective action.[7]

My brother Fran grew up on those kinds of statements,
and he believed them. So, when he was drafted to fight in the
Vietnam War, like many young men of his generation he accepted his "personal responsibility" and took "effective action." He refused to go, and ended up doing two years of
alternative service in a home for delinquent youth.

His home parish was a post-Vatican II liberal Catholic congregation that would certainly subscribe to the statements
above. Even though the pastor was a former military chaplain,
he supported Fran's application for conscientious objector status. At one point the entire parish ran a fund-raising drive and
bought a station wagon for the youth home.

But that war went on for many years until it finally faded
away. Now, fifteen years later, my brother Mike and his age
group face the same decision about registering for the draft
that Fran had to make, and the congregation is still encourag-
ing its young people to make a personal stand.

Yet the congregation has done nothing—collectively—
about either issue, war or draft. Individual members are still
encouraged to be politically active, but there is no program to
move the entire congregation into that arena.

The situation is not much different in other Catholic, Jewish and Protestant congregations in America. They continue to

spur their members on to be involved, even though any political analysis would conclude that such isolated effort, unsupported by the power of the institution, is doomed to failure and disillusionment.

ACTION BY RESOLUTION

Some congregations, sensing the inadequacy of the social service approach and the unfairness and ultimate inefficacy of the call for individual activism, follow their denominational leaders into the biggest activism trap of all: action by resolution.

I once sat at a meeting of my parish council and listened for one hour as the council members discussed a resolution condemning a new TV program that interviewed married couples in their bedrooms about their sex lives. There were many arguments about morality, freedom of speech, art and permissiveness. Nobody pointed out that the passage of such a resolution would have absolutely no effect. It was finally tabled and forgotten. Everyone's time was wasted—except that of the people producing the offending show.

Fr. Andrew Greeley, addressing his fellow Catholics through his syndicated column, made the point in his usual acerbic way:

> One of the bad effects of the ecumenical movement is that Catholics have started passing resolutions, a behavior pattern that had formerly been limited to Protestants and Jews.
>
> In the old days, when there was a Catholic meeting, no one proposed resolutions because there was enough residual immigrant street smarts in the Catholic mind to know that voting on resolutions was an utter waste of time.
>
> Now the children and the grandchildren of the precinct people are rapidly catching up with their Protestant and Jewish counterparts in the number of

pointless resolutions enthusiastically endorsed every year. . . .

Voting on resolutions is a form of "cheap grace," a way of getting a moral "kick" without doing anything.

Passing resolutions absolves those who have voted for them from the need to do anything more.[8]

If, instead of passing a meaningless resolution, the council would organize the five thousand families that make up my parish to boycott the sponsor of an offensive show, it might get some attention. If all the families in the diocese of Brooklyn and Queens would boycott, it almost certainly would get action. If the members of all Catholic, Protestant and Jewish congregations in the New York City area would join in, a program like that would be off the air fast.

But congregations aren't organized to pull off such an action. They don't think about themselves in those terms. A resolution that changes nothing is the best that they think they can do.

These resolutions do, however, have one effect. They anger the people in the congregation who disagree with them, don't understand them, didn't vote on them, or don't think that a religious congregation should be messing in "politics."

So action by resolution is ineffective, counter-productive and self-destructive.

ELECTORAL POLITICS

The final activism trap into which many congregations fall is active involvement in partisan, electoral politics. Catholic, Jewish and Protestant congregations have all been guilty of this mistake at various times and places in this country. The Moral Majority—basically a fundamentalist Protestant movement—is only the most recent example of this phenomenon and has had special impact because so many of its followers were formerly non-voters.

The problem with members of the Moral Majority is not that they are religious activists. Their problem is that they have been seduced by electoral politics.

At least theirs is a logical approach to take to activism, because on the surface it looks as though that is where a congregation can really be effective. However, there are several reasons why it is a mistake.

First, it is almost impossible to hold politicians accountable for election promises. Richard Nixon was elected in 1968 in large part because he promised that he had a "secret plan" for ending the Vietnam War. In fact he did not, but four years later he was re-elected by a huge majority. Politicians count on the electorate's short memory and need to choose the lesser of two evils when they make promises they have either no intention or no hope of keeping.

Second, religious congregations are too susceptible to "single-issue" morality appeals from candidates. Crafty politicians who promise to oppose abortion, support Israel, or favor tuition tax credits can often demand blind electoral allegiance from constituents despite stands on other issues of economy or justice antithetical to the interests of those same voters.

Third, much of modern electioneering has nothing to do with issues at all, but rather is in the hands of media image-makers. The widespread use of television to reach voters makes it almost impossible to organize congregations around issues. It means, quite simply, that the members will not follow the leaders of the congregation but rather will vote on their perceived image of the candidates presented through the media.

Fourth, electoral politics will eventually split the congregations as similar candidates appeal for their support and people make their choices on the basis of image, style, connection . . . or patronage.

Fifth, there is always the problem of what to do when a congregation's candidates lose. The pursuit of justice cannot be put on "hold" for several years. Winning candidates must be worked with. Similarly, when candidates backed by the congregation win, they will almost certainly have to make political and pragmatic compromises with other segments of their constituency that will put the congregation in the uncomfortable position of either disowning the now-elected officials or supporting them in policies untenable to the congregation.

Sixth, involvement in electoral politics is the one form of activism that will open religious congregations to harassment on their tax exempt status.

Finally, and most critically, the whole mystique of electoral politics maintains that decisions on most issues are made by elected officials and not by corporate managers, bureaucrats, union leaders, institutional heads and others who never face an election. A congregation involved in electoral politics propagates this myth and thus does a serious disservice to its members.

On a practical basis—for what it produces, the problems it causes, and the possibilities it precludes—electoral politics is a form of activism that congregations would do well to avoid.

Where does all this leave congregational activism? If none of these traditional methods is correct, then perhaps the congregation is justified in retreating into a form of spiritual pietism.

What is needed, however, is not resignation and defeat, but rather a form of activism that will actually work, that will produce results, that will make strategic sense to the overwhelming majority of the members of the congregation. That means that the approach will have to be rooted in the tradition, culture, economy, politics, and religious diversity of the place in which it is tried.

In Poland, it might mean support for the Solidarity Trade Union. In South America, it might mean formation of basic ecclesial communities. In South Africa, it might mean radical opposition to apartheid. In Israel or Iran or Nicaragua, it might mean direct involvement with the running of the state.

In the United States, the best answer to the question of religious activism is the direct, corporate, congregational involvement in community organization. Community organization can avoid the pitfalls of the other approaches to activism while remaining solidly inside the experience of American congregations.

For the congregation, involvement in the community organization process is an uncomfortable necessity.

"Uncomfortable" because it forces the congregation to deal with hard questions: self-interest, power, organization, alliances, controversy and leadership. A "necessity" because it is the best way for congregations to effectively fulfill the biblical mandate: "Fill the earth and conquer it."

Chapter 2

SELF-INTEREST: CAN YOU LOVE OTHERS IF YOU DON'T LOVE YOURSELF?

Yahweh Sabaoth, the God of Israel, says this to all the exiles deported from Jerusalem to Babylon, "Build houses, settle down; plant gardens and eat what they produce; take wives and have sons and daughters so that these can bear sons and daughters in their turn; you must increase there and not decrease. Work for the good of the country to which I have exiled you; pray to Yahweh on its behalf, since on its welfare yours depends. . . ."

Jeremiah 29:4–9

Let's assume that the leaders of a congregation are committed to activism—spiritually, theologically and practically. Let's even suppose that they're ready to try an innovative, exciting approach to revitalizing the world.

18

Off those leaders march to battle, only to turn around and discover that their people are no longer with them. Either their fellow congregants are ignoring them or—worse—are organizing a counter-revolution.

It happened in the civil rights movement; it happened in the anti-war movement; it happens every day in every community in this country where leaders of congregations get too far out in front of their members. And the results are predictable: disillusionment and burn-out on the part of the leaders and anger and confusion on the part of the followers . . . and very little real change taking place.

APATHY

Talk to clergy and lay leaders about the life of their church or synagogue, and the word that comes back most often is "apathy." Nothing is happening because people are "apathetic." How do we overcome "apathy"?

As with most words that are thrown around promiscuously, "apathy" is a good one to look up in the dictionary. It comes from the Greek word for "not feeling." But few are actually accusing their fellow congregants of being unfeeling automatons. What is usually meant is that people don't care about what the accuser thinks they *should* care about. Therefore, they are "apathetic."

This blame is really placed in exactly the wrong place. If members of a congregation are apathetic—about activism or liturgy or theology or stewardship—it is not their fault. It is their leaders' fault. Those leaders do not understand self-interest.

Most people reserve ninety-nine percent of their time and energy for pretty basic things: their family, their job, their home, their immediate neighborhood, sometimes their church or synagogue, their hobbies. If they have anything left after taking care of all that, they might be slightly interested in city or state affairs, occasionally in a major national issue or two, and—only in times of great upheaval—in some international situation.

Leaders who do not understand this will find themselves in the position of the priest in Ignazio Silone's novel, *Bread and Wine:*

"... But before I go I'd like to have a better idea of what you think about things," said Don Paolo.

"We're farmers," said Daniele. "There's not much to think about."

"Even a peasant thinks sometimes," said the priest. "Daniele, just to get things started, couldn't you tell me what you think of the situation?"

"What situation do you mean?" said Daniele. ...

"I meant the conditions of life in general here and elsewhere in Italy. What do you think of those?"

"Nothing," said Daniele. "You know, everyone has his own problems."

"Everyone has his own fleas," said Sciatap. "According to you, should we worry about someone else's fleas?"

"Everyone has his own little plot of land," said Grascia. "Everyone thinks day and night of this piece of land, whether it rains too much, whether it hails, or whether it doesn't rain at all. ..."

"You didn't understand me," said the priest. "I wanted to know what you think of the present government."

"Nothing," said Daniele.

The others agreed. "Nothing."

"Why is that?" said the priest. "You're always complaining."

"Everyone has his problems," said Magascia. "We don't care about other people's. We're interested in what's around us. We look at our neighbor's lands and vineyards. If his door or window is open, we look through and watch him eating his soup."

"Everyone has his fleas," said Sciatap. "Probably

even the government has them. And it does just what we do—it scratches. What else can we say?"

"You didn't understand me," said the priest. "I wanted to know what you thought of taxes, prices, the draft and other laws."

... When he got back to his room, he took from his suitcase the papers entitled "On the Peasant's Lack of Political Capacity" and sat at the table. He remained for a long time with his head between his hands, thinking. Finally he began to write. "Perhaps they are right."[9]

If congregational leaders ignore their followers' daily concerns or imply that they are "unimportant" or "not the concern of religion," they are going to uncover the very apathy that they constantly bemoan.

Pastor Stephen Bouman put it this way in his doctoral dissertation *Toward Politically Informed Love*:

How often have we not observed church meetings at which the "church's business" is discussed. The discussion ranges from the color of the candles to the replacement of a boiler, from kids squalling during the sermon to stewardship drives. After the meeting we see our members in little clusters in the corner, or on the steps or out on the street. Often they are discussing concerns which had no place on the agenda of the church's business: the latest break-in or mugging, a raise in taxes, their kids' school, the garbage in the streets, a local fire, a dangerous traffic corner, the hassles on their jobs. There is no reason why these real concerns of people, this "self-interest," should not be a part of their church's business. There is no reason why these concerns should not be used as a starting point to engage our people in active participation in the welfare of the city, in creation of their own history.[10]

A clear, non-romantic understanding of self-interest is a prerequisite for motivating people to do anything. To get people where you want them to be, you have to start where they are.

Moses understood this. His formula for getting the Hebrews moving after centuries of oppression in Egypt was to quote Yahweh's promise to them of a land flowing with milk and honey: ". . . if you obey my voice and hold fast to my covenant, you of all the nations shall be my very own, for all the earth is mine. I will count you a kingdom of priests, a consecrated nation" (Ex 19:5–6).

Paul certainly understood that his own salvation as well as that of others depended on his ability to reach others on terms they could understand. "I made myself all things to all men in order to save some at any cost; and I still do this, for the sake of the gospel, to have a share in its blessings" (1 Cor 9:22–23).

Even Jesus put his call for ultimate altruism in terms of self-interest: "For anyone who wants to save his life will lose it; but anyone who loses his life for my sake, and for the sake of the gospel, will save it. What gain, then, is it for a man to win the whole world and ruin his life?" (Mk 8:35–37).

Why do modern American congregational leaders think they can organize their people any other way than by addressing self-interest?

SELF-INTEREST, SELFISHNESS, ALTRUISM

What usually immobilizes leaders from understanding and using self-interest to motivate their followers to action is a confusion of it with two closely related motivations: selfishness and altruism.

When I was in Catholic grade school, we were forever ransoming "pagan babies." We would collect money and send it to missionaries who ran orphanages in foreign lands. The going rate then was about five dollars per baby.

In and of itself, the practice of sending money to the missions is not bad. Nor is there anything wrong with raising the consciousness of middle-class children about the needs of others in faraway countries.

But, to confess, the real reason we kids contributed our pennies, dimes, quarters—even dollar bills if necessary—was that whoever raised the most money got to give the baptismal name to the pagan baby being "ransomed."

This practice was merely a minor example of how the Church properly uses self-interest to motivate and teach its members. As children, we had much more need of gaining the approbation of our fellow students, parents, priests, and teachers and of winning the honor of naming some never-to-be-seen baby than we had need of understanding world economic justice.

Few would consider such a practice evil or even manipulative. For it was not an appeal to selfishness—any more than it was really an appeal to altruism—but merely an understanding of human nature that made it work.

If our teachers were trying to teach selfishness, they would have shown us how to keep the money for ourselves or at least our home parish. If they were trying to teach altruism, they would never have created a contest and a prize. But—consciously or not—the Church was teaching us that our needs were fulfilled in relationship with others: we would feel good and be recognized only by helping others.

So we ransomed the pagan babies not out of selfishness—only to help ourselves—nor out of altruism—only to help others. We did it because it was in our self-interest, which is a dialectic between the two.

Yet when the basic observation is made by an organizer that a local congregation should start its involvement in activism by understanding and addressing the self-interest of its members, charges of selfishness and irrelevancy are immediately raised by some of the very leaders who claim to want to move the congregation into action and who accuse their fellow members of being apathetic.

In the early 1970's, a coalition of community organizations in Minneapolis and St. Paul organized the "Save the Cities Campaign" to win more mortgage money for urban neighborhoods. In one of the first uses of what came to be known as the "greenlining" tactic, congregations and individuals pledged to move their bank accounts into whatever bank or savings institution would sign an agreement pledging a definite amount of loans in the Twin Cities. Such an agreement was eventually signed with the Midwest Federal Savings and Loan Association.

Not only did people and their religious institutions from all neighborhoods and economic and ethnic groups in the two cities move their money in concert because it was in their self-interest, but they were joined by suburbanites and their congregations who could see that strong central cities were vital to *their own* ability to have the kind of metropolitan area they desired.

DO-GOODERS

Haranguing, cajoling, pleading, threatening, and tricking people to get involved in broad issues of justice that they do not perceive to be in their self-interest will only succeed in producing empty pews and apathetic congregations.

Such tactics drive away the more conservative members of the congregation. Some people might respond to such techniques—at least for a while—but enlightened self-interest is the only appeal that has a chance of bringing the majority along.

How many congregations have a "social action" or "justice and peace" committee made up of an assistant pastor or rabbi and six laypeople who are involved in everything from migrant farmworkers to nuclear disarmament? Despite countless sermons and leaflets, this committee has difficulty producing more than a yawn or a paternalistic pat on the back from the rest.

There are three very good reasons for this.

First, people tend to have a healthy respect for existing institutions and leaders. For this reason, they are not about to make fools of themselves or those institutions by grabbing a picket sign and protesting every issue under the sun without—in their eyes at least—sufficient provocation.

Second, people do not like to waste their time on unattainable goals. If they don't think that they can win or at least make a difference, then they don't tend to get involved. Symbolic protest or consciousness raising holds little appeal to most congregants.

Third, people usually have a clear sense of their own self-interest. If something doesn't affect them pretty directly, they feel that they should leave it alone and let those whom it *does* affect deal with it. There are enough examples in recent years of the damage caused by paternalistic do-gooders to make the wisdom of this response seem self-evident.

Latin America's iconoclast thinker, Ivan Illich, wrote a very beautiful letter to a young woman from the United States who wanted to volunteer her time and talents to the missions of Latin America. Illich was, at the time, trying to discourage more North Americans from coming to Latin America because he felt that the Latin American Church was so aligned with the ruling classes that the missionaries could only reinforce a system that was afflicting great suffering on the common people.

Illich's "Dear Mary: Letter to an American Volunteer" is a surprise because in it he invites the young woman to come. But he urges her to please understand what she would be getting out of it: meaningful work, travel, learning, freedom:

> But please do not imagine yourself a saint or a "missioner" because you "volunteer" your services to the Church! Payment is not made in dollars alone. You forego adequate compensation in dollars because there are things you value more. For the services you offer you get exactly what you want most. You are a volunteer in the sense in which every ideal employee is one: you do what you do because you would rather do this than something else.[11]

It is that kind of clarity on self-interest that can move entire congregations into meaningful and successful activism. Do-gooders sometimes yell and scream that their fellow congregants are being dupes of the system or selfish or insensitive to the plight of others. But they would be much wiser to shut up and listen. More than self-righteousness, the reign of God needs some troops and some concrete victories. As theologian Harvey Seifert observed in his book *New Power for the Church:*

> The population of the world now desperately wants a basis for hope that goes beyond pious assertion to realistic sociological possibility. The church has unique resources for making such hope realistic—a network of buildings and paid leadership and organized groups, considerable preparatory general dedication that can be specifically focused, and a more basic, reliable, and motivating ethical perspective. There is no hope for humanity to survive major modern threats unless the typical local church moves beyond the usual handful of social activists to involve most of the congregation in powerful social witness.[12]

THREE STORIES ABOUT SELF-INTEREST

In 1972 I was trying to learn how to organize. I took a job in northeast Minneapolis—a white, ethnic working-class neighborhood. Just out of the seminary and still angry about the Vietnam War, I found myself in the midst of a patriotic, still more than slightly racist, conservative people.

There were probably twenty-five or fifty do-gooders in all of "Nordeast" (as the residents called it) who probably could have been organized into some sort of protest group around open housing or busing or the war. But I was determined to try this concept of organizing around self-interest to get the entire community moving.

That meant I had to listen to the Nordeasters. And I found that—conservative or not—they were good people and I liked them.

But I could get nothing started until I met a truck driver with a bunch of kids—a short, wizened French-American named Dan Chartraw. Dan was probably the last person in his congregation or neighborhood anybody would pick to become an activist.

However, his self-interest was immediately threatened by the federal government's plans to build a six-lane interstate highway connection—I-335—through Nordeast and within spitting distance of Chartraw's house.

So together we organized the North East Community Organization and we eventually beat I-335. In order to do so, Chartraw had to cross the Mississippi River and work with some of the blacks on the north side of Minneapolis where the highway was also not wanted. That he did, and he later allowed that maybe those folks "weren't so bad" once you got to know them.

I remember the day Dan Chartraw was named "Man of the Year" by the Nordeast newspaper. It was probably one of the greatest days of his life.

In 1974 I was hired to organize a group in DuPage County, Illinois. DuPage lies directly west of Chicago, and at the time it had the fourth highest per capita income of any county in the country. It was to Illinois Republicans what Daley's Chicago was to Democrats: home.

Again, there were a few do-gooders who were ready to take on the problems of the universe immediately, but I spent a lot of time listening to the self-interest of the people all over DuPage.

Joe and Dorothy Schutz were two of them. They were native Chicagoans who had moved in their later years to their dream home in the suburbs. Neither of them was the radical type; they could have been anybody's grandparents.

But the Schutzes had one problem. Their beautiful house

was near a creek, and there was so much development going on in the flood plains of DuPage that every time there was a good rain the Schutzes had to row to their home.

So when the DuPage Citizens Organization launched its "Flood Land Action Campaign" (F.L.A.C.), Joe Schutz was one of its chairmen. Developers, who wanted to continue to build suburban housing tracts and shopping centers on the flood plains, fought to protect their traditional prerogatives to do with their property whatever they desired. After a long and acrimonious fight, the DuPage county board finally passed a model flood plain ordinance limiting construction in these areas.

I'll never forget Joe Schutz's face the day the ordinance passed. "We beat the bastards," he said simply.

In 1976 I moved to Pittsburgh to start a new organizing drive there. Fr. John Unger, the distinguished, sixty-year-old pastor of Sacred Heart Church in the Shadyside neighborhood, was the reluctant chairman of the Sponsoring Committee. Fr. Unger was never too sure that he wanted himself or his parish to be involved in something quite so "radical" as the Metropolitan Citizens Organization. But he was trying to respond to Vatican II's call for congregations to get involved in their community, and this approach seemed to make some sense to him—although he was careful to let his young assistant, Fr. Bill Hausen, do the front work.

We fought and stopped a mob-connected nightclub—the "Fantastic Plastic"—from opening in his parish, but Fr. Unger didn't like all the controversy involved, especially when one of the principals called and threatened him.

But when the organization took on the Pittsburgh Board of Education and forced it to sell a large tract of unused land inside his parish to a developer, Fr. Unger suddenly saw the concrete benefits of the community organization to his congregation.

Homes are up on that site now and filled with new members of Sacred Heart Church and other congregations in the neighborhood. Fr. Unger has retired, but I know that he still looks back on those organizing days as an important chapter in his ministry.

FROM HERE TO THERE

These stories are nice, even inspiring. There are other stories which are not so nice and rather discouraging. Even in each of the above cases, people won important issues but lost the organization in the sense that they were not able to sustain it as a permanent fixture on the political scene in those communities. Part of that failure was my lack of experience or skill as an organizer, and part was the failure of the local congregations to see the value of the organization to their long-term institutional self-interest.

Still, the lives of many individuals were touched. Some grew, others retreated. One thing is sure: none of them—individuals or their congregations—would have even tried to reshape their world if the leaders and the organizers hadn't been willing to deal with self-interest.

The critics of this approach charge that such organizing leads to narrowness, self-centeredness, even racism. They claim that such activism never leads to a broader understanding of institutional and global injustice. My experience is this: sometimes it does, and sometimes it does not.

When an elderly black woman, Mrs. Rosa Parks, sat down in the "whites only" section of the bus in Montgomery, Alabama over twenty years ago, she was merely operating in her self-interest: she was tired, the seat was empty, and her dignity would not allow her to stand. Mrs. Parks had no intention of starting a bus boycott or launching the modern civil rights movement, but that was the effect of her acting in her own behalf.

The questions about the level of Rosa Parks' consciousness at the time or whether she eventually became an enlightened advocate of international justice is not important. The important thing is that she acted in her own self-interest, and in so doing acted in the interest of her entire society.

People can still remain caught in their parochialism and prejudices and passivity—even if they do get involved in local issues that affect them. But I am willing to say that people will never reach any higher level of understanding of activism if they do not start with issues that do affect them directly. It is an "only if, but not necessarily" situation.

In his important book *An American Strategic Theology,* Fr. John Coleman frames the question thus:

> At the local level, programs of community organizers have done much to enlighten parishioners about the locus of power in their communities and issues such as redlining practices of banks and inadequate sanitation and services. I know of no local church programs so effective in making a first start toward achieving what the Latin Americans call "conscientization" as community organizing programs in neighborhoods. I also know of no other strategy in the American Catholic Church so creative for social justice. If ever there was an instance of what Weber called "elective affinity," it is that between community organization and the issues of the neighborhood and a parish. For parishes and neighborhoods—at least in inner cities—stand or fall together. The danger is that this splendid vehicle for empowerment at local levels is capable of its own version of "tactical provincialism" which fails to join the issues where people are hurting to a wider social analysis of national and international structures of injustice.[13]

Community organization offers the local congregation a vehicle for getting people started in activism because it starts with the self-interest of its members. It deals with issues that are local and winnable. It cuts across liberal, moderate and conservative lines.

Once the congregation gets into action, there is nothing that must stop it from seeing its interest in larger and larger arenas and from seeing the connection between issues on a local level and those on a national or even international scale.

That wider perspective is admittedly a long way down the road. Some will never make it. But that does not negate the value and the correctness of beginning.

Chapter 3

POWER: GOOD INTENTIONS ARE NOT ENOUGH

The kingdom of God is not just words; it is power.

1 Corinthians 4:20

The pursuit and use of power is the other stumbling block—in addition to the concept of self-interest—to American congregational activism . . . and for some very good reasons.

In our lifetimes, Americans have seen the misuse of power in the political sphere, the corporate world, labor unions, even religious bodies themselves. With this kind of experience, it is not hard to understand why congregations would duck the minute the word "power" is mentioned. We all have Lord Acton's formula firmly in memory: "Power tends to corrupt, and absolute power corrupts absolutely. Great men are almost always bad men."

And yet there is an equally obvious truth that without power we have no ability to make our vision of the way the world should be a reality, no way to defend our values. Webster defines "power" as nothing more and nothing less than the "capacity to act."

So a congregation committed to helping to create the world—to *act*-ivism—has little choice but to seek power for itself and its people.

Pastor Richard Johnson saw the dilemma this way in his monograph *Reflections on Self-Interest and Power: A Theological Justification for Community Organization:*

> We must examine, therefore, our aversion to the use of power . . . it is the realization that power means responsibility. If I have power, I am obligated to use it on the behalf of good. I deny the existence of my power lest I be called on to employ it. Thus the flight from power is really the flight from responsibility.[14]

AMERICAN DEMOCRACY

Let us first analyze Lord Acton's troublesome aphorism in the context of American political theory. To begin, no one is proposing absolute power for local congregations. History has proven the danger of absolute rulers—especially of the "religious" variety. The worry in this case is ludicrous, however. The problem is not whether American congregations have too much power. In most cases they have none at all.

This leaves them out of the U.S. system of checks and balances envisioned by people like James Madison in *The Federalist Papers* and commented upon by astute observers of the American democratic experiment like Alexis de Tocqueville and Jacques Maritain. Maritain wrote in *Reflections on America:*

> There is in this country a swarming multiplicity of particular communities—self-organized groupings, associations, unions, sodalities, vocational or religious brotherhoods, in which men join forces with one another at the elementary level of their everyday concerns and interests. . . .
>
> Such basic organized multiplicity . . . is, in my opinion, a particularly favorable condition for the sound development of democracy. . . .[15]

Our forebears saw that democracy would only work as long as the various self-interest groupings—from merchants to farmers to churchpeople—were kept in balance, with no group gaining dominance or feeling that its basic needs were not being met by the democratic process.

To insure that desired equilibrium, each group had to be organized and have its share of the power. Any group left out—by design or accident—would provide the discontent to undermine the republic.

Groups that have felt so dispossessed—blacks, industrial workers, Hispanics, women—have had to organize massive protest movements to claim their share of the American dream. And in each case, many national religious bodies and local congregations supported and joined that effort.

With modern society effecting the destruction of basic family and spiritual values, local congregations have little choice but to organize to insure that their values are given a respected place in the democratic mix.

Neo-liberals like economist Lester Thurow argue that such self-interest groups only have the power to delay decisions from being made rather than the power to actually obtain their own goals. Thus, Thurow argues in *The Zero Sum Society* that we have arrived at a state of political paralysis, with each self-interest group negating the aspirations of the others:

> With everyone being protected, there are no concerned, disinterested citizens to make the democratic process work. Special-interest lobbies dominate, and all belong to some special interest. The ability to decide collapses into lengthy adversary procedures where everyone is worn out and no one is the long-run winner. Costs rise, new projects cannot be undertaken, and old projects cannot be transformed.[16]

This paralysis is much too contemporary a situation for Thurow to draw his conclusion that self-interest organization is not the best basis for democracy. Where in this country's two hundred year history have been the "concerned, disinterested citizens to make the democratic process work"? This is a myth taught by high school social studies teachers—and too many religious congregations.

Historically, it has been self-interest groups that have been able to guarantee that their agendas are included in any national consensus. Social security, women's suffrage, civil rights and labor legislation are but a few examples where groups caused change beneficial to the entire body politic because of their organized action on their own behalf.

Although Thurow may be correct about the immediate national malaise, what he fails to understand or admit is that such veto power exercised by any group is a prior condition for its participation in any consensus that must and will develop on the future of this country.

The fact that most religious groups do not have even the negating power of business, labor, farmer, military, civil rights and other interest groups shows just how far they have fallen out of the democratic experiment.

The statement that power "tends to corrupt" is true, and no organized group in America is untainted in some way. Only those who are unorganized—and therefore do nothing—are pure.

Rabbi Emil Fachenheim described the two-edged sword that is power in his article "A Jewish View of Religious Responsibility for the Social Order":

> All social organization involves power. But power is amoral before it can be made moral, and presumably it always retains aspects of amorality and even immorality.... (Religious people) may either forswear all use of power, in order to remain true to the prophetic imperative. But then they condemn their own efforts to ineffectiveness.... Alternatively, they may seek power for the sake of the prophetic imperative which demands realization. But then they must recognize that they become compromised in its use; and their religious motivation is no protection against such compromise.[17]

We often fail to distinguish between power's use and its abuse. Power tends to corrupt, as does money, sex, good looks and television. It means that people of good will must be careful and reflective about what they are doing—and why. As Pastor Johnson points out, "... the failure of people to use their power inevitably increases the power of those who already possess power. The failure to use power is therefore irresponsible, cowardly, and—again—complicity in the injustices of society."[18]

And if "great men are almost always bad men," it only makes it more imperative that families and congregations trying to provide role models for their young get cracking in substituting a few good ones of their own.

VALUES

Are "values" really values if we are not willing to act on them and fight for them? Louis Raths, Merrill Harmin and Sidney Simon—three classroom teachers who have struggled with that question in their book *Values and Teaching*—feel that such action is part of the very definition of the word:

> Where we have a value, we believe it should show up in aspects of our living, in our behavior. We may do some reading about things we value. We may form friendships or join organizations that nourish our values. We may spend money on values. We very likely budget time or energy for them. In short, for a value to be present, life itself must be affected. Nothing can be a value that does not, in fact, give direction to actual living. The person who talks about something but never does anything about it is acting from something other than a value, in our definition.[19]

An obvious example today is the professional couple who try to teach their children that spiritual and human relation values are the most important things in life, but who never have time for each other, their family, their friends or their congregation. No matter what that couple *says* about its values, it is clear to everyone—especially their children—that money and the things it can buy or their professional prestige or their interesting work is what they really value.

Take the case of Fr. George Clements, a black Catholic priest in Chicago. As a direct result of his values and his preaching of those values, Fr. Clements adopted a young black boy. He then challenged—with apparent success—black families to do the same. The wisdom of the celibate priest's act can be debated forever, but few will argue that he did not truly believe in his values.

Numerous studies have documented the breakdown of the family as a center of values. Most theories blame subjective psychological, social or spiritual lack or failure on the part of the families themselves. Few look to the objective, outside pressures on the family unit. Christopher Lasch identified this as one of the phenomena of "the culture of narcissism."[20]

In its pamphlet *Organizing for Family and Congregation*, the Industrial Areas Foundation took this position:

> The intermediate voluntary institutions—including churches—are ineffectual in a power relationship with the powerful. As a result, the middle is collapsing, confused. The economic and political middle of this country is being sucked dry by a vacuum—a vacuum of power and values. Into that vacuum have moved the huge corporations, mass media and "benevolent" government. Those institutions in large part created the vacuum because the churches and unions were not prepared for the new institutional arrangements and technologies that have overwhelmed us since World War II. So we have given over control of much of our lives (including many tasks formerly exercised by families) to "experts" and "specialists," who are in fact only fronts for institutions of greed

and unaccountable power. Without effective institutional power of their own, the families and churches withdraw, backbite, blame each other, or perhaps experiment with fads—ignoring their history and strength.[21]

On economics alone, the family is being crushed. In real dollars, the average family's income has actually declined in the last ten years. Yet the demands of an advertising-induced consumer mentality have sent both parents into the workplace—one or both often working two jobs. Debt at double-digit interest rates has turned many families into little more than money-generating machines.

Cultural forces like television and drugs come armed with a sophistication and technology that the average family is unprepared to combat.

Meanwhile, the family sees its neighborhood deteriorate, its schools fail, transportation grind to a halt and crime rates soar.

The results of this pressure on the family are predictable: fighting, alcoholism, drug addiction, divorce, delinquency, abuse. It is not surprising that the family sees itself in a battle over values that has already been lost. And rather than becoming an ally in the battle, too often the congregation becomes one more source of negative judgment and pressure.

The family has no power to challenge the vast institutions of economics, culture and government that are doing it in. Just as the Hallihans and the Chartraws and the Schutzes needed help against the gas company or the highway department or the developers, every family needs a mediating institution that it can trust to aid in the ongoing power struggle over values. For most people, that institution could be the congregation.

Consider: the congregation shares most basic values with its families and has their trust; the congregation has the resources to help (especially if it will ally with like-minded groups); and the congregation has the theological basis for involvement.

However, in order to do more good than harm for the family, the congregation must be competent. That means that it must figure out how to acquire enough "capacity to act" to be helpful.

POWER ANALYSIS

Neophyte activists make the mistake of getting into fights that they have no chance of winning or attacking targets that have no power to resolve their issue or using tactics that do not have the slightest effect on their opponent. All of these errors stem from the same failure: the inability to develop an accurate power analysis.

Power analysis has two sides: theirs and yours. On the one hand, an organization must learn how to determine who holds the power to grant its demands. On the other, the organization must be very clear about how much power it realistically does or does not possess at any particular point in time.

A power analysis is simply a large sheet of paper. A really good one might cover the entire wall of an organization's headquarters. On this paper are three things:

1. *Names* of all the major institutions or individuals who do—or possibly could—influence the decisions being made about a particular community. So, obviously, there would be the mayor and the governor, the major banks and utilities, landlords and real estate agents, etc. Perhaps not so obviously, there would also be campaign contributors and stockholders, organized crime figures and drug pushers, bishops and civil rights leaders—in short, everyone with power. Also on the analysis would be the local congregations and the nascent community organization.

2. *Circles* around each name indicating by their size the relative strength of each of the names on the paper. In many ways, this determination is a subjective guess based on the perceived power of each, and it certainly changes according to which issue is being discussed. As the organization gets more

sophisticated, it becomes possible to accurately estimate how much weight each character is going to swing at a particular time on a specific question.

3. *Lines* between each of the names, indicating where relationships occur and what the nature of the relationship—both positive and negative—might be. If a particular landlord was a major contributor to the mayor's last campaign, it is important to know that fact before seeing the mayor about the landlord's alleged nefarious activities in the community. What will very quickly happen on such a power analysis is that many lines will begin to emanate from a few power sources. Those will be the power brokers in the community and the ones that the organization must engage if it is to be successful.

This power analysis is a growing, vibrant instrument that the community organization uses to plan its action. It tells both where the fight must be taken and who the potential allies on a particular issue might be. It is a guide to action, not—as some have it—an end in itself.

For example, in DuPage County, Illinois, the DuPage Citizens Organization used its power analysis to discover that the county treasurer was depositing county funds in banks in return for personal loans to fund his various property investments. The organization then began to play the banks and the county board against the treasurer until he was eventually removed from office and sent to jail.

A power analysis is developed by observing how things actually get done—not how they are supposed to happen. Nothing is more frustrating to observe than a well-meaning citizens group sitting through an interminable public hearing on an issue important to its community and knowing that the decision is being made across the street in the offices of someone with no formal standing in the debate: a major realtor, a well-connected lawyer, a powerful media consultant.

It is not that difficult to obtain this information. There are plenty of sources that are willing to help others understand how things work. It is also important to learn how to read a newspaper: saving obscure articles that make connections or reading between the lines for what a reporter is trying to say but the editor won't allow. The best additions to the power analysis are those made by the organization itself. As various issues get resolved, the relationship between various players becomes very clear: how they refer to each other, who supports whom on a particular controversy, who does whom in. If these connections are duly noted on the developing power analysis, the organization—and its member congregations—will over time begin to get an accurate picture of how decisions are really made in their community, and what power is necessary to amass in order to be heard.

ONE EXAMPLE OF POWER

If you leave the gleaming new office buildings in downtown Pittsburgh developed with considerable public and corporate money and effort in "Renaissance I and II" and travel into the neighborhoods, you will discover the workers and their families who built the industry that made the city possible.

What the Pittsburgh power structure did to the Bloomfield/Garfield neighborhood shows the unacceptability of leaving the future of one's community to the whim of others.

Starting with the building of a huge low-income high rise right in the middle of a single family residential community, followed by an abortive housing inspection program that drove many long-time residents out, and continued with a systematic withdrawal of city services, Bloomfield/Garfield headed in the direction of many urban neighborhoods: total devastation.

A creative and courageous priest, Fr. Leo Henry—the pastor of St. Lawrence O'Toole Catholic parish—decided to fight back. Fr. Henry turned to community organization as the neighborhood's only hope.

His first action was a Candidates Night in the parish hall where he turned out more people and more politicians than Bloomfield/Garfield had seen in decades. That night, war was declared and the Bloomfield/Garfield Corporation was born.

Mass rallies, demonstrations and periodic invasions of city hall became the order of the day. Slowly, the neighborhood began to receive the attention and services it needed.

There is in Garfield a main street—Penn Avenue—a once-vibrant business district full of little shops that was in decline like so many similar strips in U.S. cities. Part of the reason for its demise was the decision of major retailers and financial institutions to move to more lucrative suburban malls.

Fr. Henry turned his focus onto Penn Avenue and decided that it would never come back without a bank. He was right, but when he asked my opinion as the organizer for the group, I felt that they did not yet have enough power—and possibly never would—to get a bank to move back in. I suggested that maybe the organization should look into starting a credit union.

"No way," insisted Fr. Henry. "We don't need some rinky-dink credit union; we need a full service bank. We'll just have to put the pressure on the banks the way we have been doing on city hall."

I pointed out to Fr. Henry that banks do not exactly respond to protest groups and demonstrations the same way that politicians do. If he wanted to get a bank on Penn Avenue, he could do it only one way: play the various elements on the organization's power analysis off against one another.

And so he did. With organizer Patrick Battel of the staff of the Metropolitan Citizens Organization and with leaders like Marie Miller and Aggie Brose and Al Heyl and Pat Maloney, the Bloomfield/Garfield Corporation organized every person and institution and business in their neighborhood to pledge to move all of their banking business to whatever bank would move onto Penn Avenue. They had about $2.5 million pledged.

We knew from talking with bankers that that was not enough, so they went after the county government and got it to pledge $3 million in public funds. Then the city government did the same.

Finally, they called in the bankers.

The negotiations were held in front of five hundred people. The choice quickly came down to the two biggest banks in western Pennsylvania, Mellon and Equibank—neither of whom wanted to lose the deposits or the public relations value of being chosen as the "bank that was responsive to the community." By this time, both were desperately looking for space to rent on Penn Avenue.

Mellon arrogantly threatened to open a branch on the strip whether it had an agreement with the organization or not.

Equibank saw a chance to score a publicity coup over Mellon and treated the neighborhood leaders seriously and with respect.

Not surprisingly, the organization voted for Equibank. An agreement was signed, the branch opened, people moved their money, the bank began to make loans to families and businesses in the area, and the neighborhood continued to make a comeback.

This was real organization, real power, and real change.

And it could never have been done without the involvement of the local congregation, which provided the initiative, financial support, credibility, leadership, meeting space and spiritual basis for the organizing effort.

Chapter 4

ORGANIZATION: YOU CAN'T NEGOTIATE WITH A MOVEMENT

After this, Moses and Aaron went to Pharaoh and said to him, "This is what Yahweh, the God of Israel, has said, 'Let my people go, so that they may keep a feast in the wilderness in honor of me.'" "Who is Yahweh," Pharaoh replied, "that I should listen to him and let Israel go? I know nothing of Yahweh, and I will not let Israel go."

Exodus 5:1–2

Even congregations that decide to seek power as the means to defend their families and communities often do not know how to get it. Power is obtained through organization.

Throughout history, when people have wanted something badly enough, when they have become tired of being abused, when their basic values have been threatened, they organize. They create organizations of different sizes and shapes: governments, armies, corporations, political parties, unions, agencies, societies, dioceses, congregations.

In "Some Reflections on the Catholic Experience in the United States," historian David O'Brien comments:

> For all our talk of the Christian social order thirty years ago and of personalism and liberation today, our programs are best and most effective when they accept and work with the pluralistic, interest group structures which our marketplace mentality has created. The church needs to provide a support system for its ethnic, Chicano, and black members, but they in turn must realize the lesson of the past. Until they get their own people together and generate common goals and collective institutions, they are not going to make it. In America, nobody else does it for you. The name of the game in the market is power. Nobody ever really shares it willingly; they share it when those on the other side are capable of forcing them to do so.[22]

In a local, geographically defined area—whether that be a large neighborhood, a section of a city, or a metropolitan area—one way through which a congregation can seek to increase its power is community organization. Community organization is an attempt to combine existing civic, religious, business, union, service, and volunteer organizations in a particular area into a new vehicle that can negotiate with other power institutions for the self-interest of its members.

These kinds of organizations have several important characteristics that differentiate them from other citizen organizing efforts.

1. *Leadership.* The leadership of a good community organization is not based on one person, but operates as a collective

with decisions reached democratically and key functions inter-
changeable among many people. This prevents the effort from
becoming dependent on a single person or being subverted by
that leader's departure or political ambitions. The leadership
of a community organization should be well trained in the
skills needed to run a large organization. Rather than steal the
best leaders from the congregation, the community organization should produce new leaders that are helpful not only to
the community, but also to the congregation itself.

2. *Membership.* The membership of a community organization is not open to individuals, but rather made up of as
many existing groups in the community as possible. None
should be excluded unless they have an irreconcilable conflict
of interest (such as a political party) or do not subscribe to the
basic values of the group (such as an avowedly racist group).
Much work needs to be done with the membership to keep it
informed about the activities of the organization, so that the
membership remains disciplined and loyal to the organization
in the midst of controversy.

3. *Issues.* The community organization must be capable of
handling several issues at one time. This broadens both its appeal and its effectiveness. At the same time, however, the organization should be very careful to pick issues that it has
enough power to do something about in a reasonable amount
of time. Most of its member groups will not have time or patience for quixotic or symbolic protests. Their concern—and
the reason they will join the community organization in the
first place—is to win concrete victories that provide real relief
to their families and neighborhoods.

4. *Action.* The community organization is in constant action. Action is what provides the victories that lay the basis for
future success, exercises the networks inside the organization,
trains the leaders, develops relationships with allies, and sup-
plies energy to the organization. This action can range from

small research teams to mass meetings of thousands of people. Organizations that try to rest on their reputation quickly find themselves forgotten in the rush of the media-oriented immediacy of modern society.

5. *Money.* The community organization must have its own money if it is going to be effective. This self-sufficiency is what gives the community organization the stability it needs to persevere in lengthy battles and the independence necessary to win significant victories. Most of this money should come from dues from its member groups, the rest from fund raising efforts. This is very important, and also very difficult, for congregations who are struggling with their own finances to understand. However, under no circumstances should the community organization take any money from the government or foundations, for they will ultimately control the organization.

MOVEMENTS AND CIVICS

Most congregations have little experience with the kind of serious community organization effort described above. If involved in any type of organization, they are usually drawn either into small civic organizations or large mass movements.

Every neighborhood has a neighborhood association or block club. These organizations are usually very small, individual membership groups concerned about very local issues like garbage collection and snow removal. They have no overview of the problems of their community or their families and make no pretense of training leaders or developing allies. They usually have no money and neither seek nor welcome congregational membership. They are almost always reactive groups and often reactionary.

In my own neighborhood in Queens, New York, the local block club association opposed plans by Catholic Charities and backed by my parish to build senior citizen housing on vacant property owned by the diocese. This opposition was based entirely on the fact that the project would receive federal subsidies and would therefore be open to people of all races from outside the neighborhood. Civic groups like this are often left the role of nay-sayers to any change because they know that they do not have enough power to control their own destiny.

Movements are also well known to members of congregations of all faiths, for their denominational leaders are always trying to get them involved in problems such as world hunger or civil rights, peace or the environment. Movements are often organized around a particular charismatic leader or a single issue or both. Again, membership is by the individual—not the congregation. Action is on the national or international level, and is often symbolic. Movements are highly dependent on the whim of the media for their existence and effectiveness. Some movements have money while they are popular but then spend the rest of their lives trying to maintain their solvency and justify their existence.

The Clergy and Laity Concerned About the War in Vietnam eventually became just the Clergy and Laity Concerned when the Vietnam conflict ended. The movement continued after its initial reason for existence was gone, and seemed to spend an inordinate amount of time defining its purpose and raising money. The same story can be repeated about many movements on all sides of the ideological spectrum.

There are also local "movements" that congregations become involved in. These are usually crises such as a crime wave or a rash of arson when everyone gets excited, attends a few hysterical meetings, and then goes back to doing whatever he or she was doing before. Politicians have a field day racing to head up these parades, because they know that there will be no organization left afterward to hold them accountable for any promise that they make.

Congregations involved in these kinds of efforts will be disappointed and disillusioned. The power that they offer is minimal and mercurial. They offer nothing back to the congregation itself. Conversely, a broad-based, multi-issue community organization—built correctly and to last—offers the congregation a chance at serious power and helps build rather than drain the resources of the congregation.

RECOGNITION

In the 1960's, I had this fantasy. The peace movement announced that ten million Americans had agreed to cancel their life insurance policies, pull all their money out of the bank, and sell all of their stocks on the same day if President Johnson did not negotiate with them a plan for ending the Vietnam War.

Under pressure from the terrified business community, Johnson agreed to negotiate. Three prominent Americans were chosen to represent the peace movement: say Dorothy Day, Rabbi Abraham Heschel and Rev. Martin Luther King, Jr. After some meetings, Johnson refused to budge. The spokespeople sent out word that—as a demonstration of their seriousness—one hundred thousand of their followers would carry out the threat the next day. They did, with predictable disruption of the economic system.

Johnson then began negotiating seriously. As the deadline approached for the massive threatened action, the president capitulated and signed an agreement to get all American troops out of Vietnam within six months on an agreed timetable. The entire ten million Americans accepted this settlement as the best possible deal that could be negotiated and called off their protest. The United States got out of Vietnam—years before it finally did in reality.

The reason that this was a fantasy is that the peace movement was not an organization: it had no universally recognized leaders who could negotiate for it; it had no disciplined members who could carry out—or call off, for that matter—tactics upon the direction of the leaders; most importantly, it was not interested in compromise or negotiated solutions. It was a cause: peace now.

Organizations, unlike movements, are after what is possible. They understand that they have limited power and that their goals and desires are often in conflict with those of other individuals and institutions which also have power.

Again, David O'Brien notes:

> When Saul Alinsky and his Catholic friends applied the union techniques to community organization, the lesson was that the city, too, was a marketplace. Unorganized people were powerless; only organization of human resources could enable groups without money or influence to play the market game in politics and society. In 1965, the war on poverty's community action program tried to transfer resources to fund community organization, but the political stakes were too high. The government was not to foster formation of new organized groups to enter the urban struggle. Alinsky, like Gompers before him, knew it all along: the only worthwhile organizations are those people build for themselves, the only worthwhile goals are those people set for themselves, the only permanent gains are those achieved through the struggles of the marketplace.[23]

For organizations, action is a means to an end. That end is recognition by existing power centers that a new element must be considered in future decisions about a particular issue or specific community. Recognition is the first step—and often the most important step—in negotiation.

Negotiation is why the basic elements of a community organization—collective leadership, disciplined membership, multi-issue, constant action and indigenous money—are so important. They provide the continuity and the impetus that gets the organization to the negotiating table.

The ability to negotiate is the reason why organization is more powerful and successful than movement, and why organization will ultimately produce more real change.

ONE EXAMPLE OF ORGANIZATION

Queens County shares the western end of Long Island with Brooklyn. Between them, the two boroughs have over five million people—well over half of the entire population of New York City. Yet in every way—culture, finance, media, public service, politics—Brooklyn and Queens are abused stepchildren of Manhattan.

Queens has been especially "blessed" by the presence of New York's two airports: LaGuardia and JFK International. These are two of the busiest airports in the world, and while they provide jobs for many Queens residents they also produce incredible problems for those residents in terms of noise, pollution, traffic congestion, crime, and encroachment into residential neighborhoods.

The Port Authority of New York and New Jersey is the prototype for the kind of quasi-governmental body created to construct and run public works projects with a minimum of interference from government and citizenry. One of its many responsibilities is to operate the New York airports under a lease from the city.

The Queens Citizens Organization (Q.C.O.) is a congregationally based organization formed in 1976 in an attempt to give the residents of Queens a vehicle for obtaining some say over the forces affecting their families and neighborhoods. It was never the position of the Queens Citizens Organization that it was against the development of JFK and LaGuardia. Such a position would have been against the self-interest of the moderate, family-oriented members of its constituent congregations. Many of those people worked in air-related industries, and for those out of work it provided one of the few hopes for economic growth in the borough. The middle class taxpayers of Queens also appreciated the revenues that derived to the city from the successful operation of the airports.

However, it was also not in the interest of the congregations to allow the historical relationship of the community to the Port Authority to continue. In the last fifty years, the explosion of air travel and air freight had caused the two airports to constantly expand both their physical and psychological boundaries into the community. Kennedy Airport itself had grown from little Idlewild Field to encompass several previously residential communities until it covered a total of five thousand acres: the size of Manhattan from 34th Street to the Battery Tunnel. Both airports now abut Queens residential communities. What is worse, industry from the airports began to creep off the airport itself—aided by Port Authority policies—filling formerly residential communities with warehouses, clogging streets and highways with trucks and cars, and ruining pavements and sewers.

If there were ever a David and Goliath situation, this was it. On the one side was the oldest, richest and most powerful public authority in the country. The Port Authority had assets of four billion dollars, a staff of eighty-five hundred, legal authority from two states, and access to the top legal, financial, media and political institutions in the world. Its offices covered several floors of the magnificent World Trade Center, overlooking five states.[24]

When it began this fight, Q.C.O. was a coalition of some twenty Catholic and Protestant churches that had only begun to work together a few years before. It struggled to make its annual budget of $100,000 to pay a staff of three and a consulting contract with the Industrial Areas Foundation. I was the lead organizer at the time. Q.C.O. was viewed with a combination of indifference and suspicion by the major institutions of power in New York—including the media. Its offices were on the third floor of an old convent at St. Thomas the Apostle Church in Woodhaven, Queens.

Q.C.O. was conceived differently from most citizen movements. It is based in congregations throughout Queens County who see it as an important part of their ministry and who pay substantial dues to keep it independent. Q.C.O. was organized with one principle in mind: to achieve enough power to be able to hold accountable—according to the values of its member congregations—the various institutions of business and government whose decisions affect Queens.

The Port Authority was one such institution. It was designed to insulate itself from just this kind of external pressure. The congregations that made up Q.C.O. had seen the destruction of their communities and families for fifty years by the unplanned and unaccountable expansion of LaGuardia and Kennedy Airports by the Port Authority. If these congregations were going to prove that the value of human needs taking priority over financial needs is real to them, then at some point they had to address this issue with action. In 1980, with Q.C.O. as their vehicle of power, that time came. Their goal was not merely to win some concessions from the Port Authority, but to effect real, long-term, institutional change in the way that the Port Authority ran the airports and related to its neighbors.

The leaders of Q.C.O. in this fight had several things in common: all were committed and active members of their various congregations; all were family and church centered; none had political aspirations; all were long-time Queens residents and chose to remain so; none were very experienced in this kind of social action; and all believed that their values required them to act.

They were the average Americans who are the backbone of this country and its congregations: Richard Ammons, a retired salesman; William Collins, a federal personnel evaluator; Gail Cruise, a student teacher; Charles Horvath, an advertising executive; Wilma Kempf, a housewife; Lorraine Lynch, a housewife; Dwayne Mau, a pastor; Owen McEntee, a retired policeman; Patricia Oettinger, a secretary; John Pettei, Jr., a banker; Marion Scott, a bus dispatcher; William Strehlow, a pastor; Patricia Troll, a housewife; Anthony Vera, a social worker; Valerie Wingo, a secretary.

These people went through hundreds of hours of meetings, planning sessions, training seminars, actions and negotiations over a two year period. During that time, they grew measurably in the skills and understanding of power. At various times they organized meetings of five hundred, one thousand, fifteen hundred and two thousand of their fellow citizens and congregation members in support of their efforts. They were interviewed by local and national print and electronic media. They defended their positions before bishops and governors and bank presidents and union leaders.

Their entire struggle was to win recognition from the Port Authority as a legitimate participant in discussions about the future plans and operation of the airports. All of their action and strategy was based on this objective.

The Port Authority first assumed that, like most protest movements, Q.C.O. could be ignored or coopted. It refused to recognize or negotiate with the organization. But because it had a solid base in the congregations of Queens, Q.C.O. was able to attract the allies that it needed—especially then Lieutenant Governor and now Governor Mario Cuomo.

Q.C.O. also had developed a fairly accurate power analysis of New York City and was able to parlay that knowledge into an impressive array of allies against the Port Authority. The key breakthrough came when Q.C.O. discovered that the Port Authority was seeking a fifteen year extension on its lease on the two airports.

Mobilizing all of its resources and allies, Q.C.O. managed to block action on the lease until the Port Authority negotiated a settlement whereby a special fund of two million dollars was set up by the Port Authority to pay for neighborhood improvements in Queens that were suggested and approved by Q.C.O.

This was not as much as Q.C.O. had hoped to win, and much more than the Port Authority had ever considered giving up. The most important victory was not the two million dollars but the implicit pledge it signified by the Port Authority to become a better neighbor and the recognition of Q.C.O. as a legitimate power that now must be consulted in decisions about the future of Queens.

For the congregations that made up Q.C.O., this issue strengthened the resolve of those who began to see possible changes in their role in Queens and the development of their own leaders.

INSTITUTIONAL CHANGE

Families need organizational power because their problems are not individual but institutional. An individual up against a utility company or a bank or city hall or a Port Authority is going to lose all but a few well-publicized cases.

Employment, housing, energy, education, marketing, health care, media, and social services have all been institutionalized to such an extent that only a rearrangement of power patterns will bring any long-term relief from the pressure on the family. Such rearrangement requires the creation and the recognition of new organizations that can negotiate for those they represent with those institutions already exercising power.

The local congregation can be the basis for such a new power distribution, as theologian J. Philip Wogamon describes in his article "The Church as a Mediating Institution: Theological and Philosophical Perspectives":

> When it is true to its nature, (the congregation) is the quintessential mediating structure in society. Religious groups are by definition the bearers of human tradition concerning ultimate meaning and value; and, by common practice, they are organized in local, face-to-face, associational form. The second linkage, that with political power structures, has been established or neglected by religious groups in a wide variety of ways through history. But the opportunity is clearly present for the church to function in that linkage, and to fulfill the role rather well.[25]

The isolated congregation, however, will soon experience many of the same problems as the individual family. To succeed in this role of mediating structure, the congregation needs a vehicle that will insert a new power element in the existing equation, much as John L. Lewis' CIO did in the 1930's on the American industrial scene, the basic ecclesial communities are now doing in South America, Henry's Bloomfield/Garfield Corporation did in Pittsburgh, or the Queens Citizens Organization is doing in New York City.

Such organizations need their own money, trained leaders and staff. They must be broad-based and multi-issue. They must develop creative tactics that will win them recognition.

And they must have their local religious congregations involved from the beginning in their development and execution.

Chapter 5

ALLIES: LEAVE THE BAGGAGE BY THE DOOR

Anyone who is not against us is for us.
Mark 9:40

Community organization offers congregations a place to practice what they preach about working with people of other faiths and denominations and colors and cultures.

One minister I know contemptuously refers to most ecumenical religious efforts as "Thanksgiving Sunrise Services." He feels that such superficial exercises pretend that there is a relationship when in fact none exists.

I attended the funeral of Monsignor Vincent Dooley at Resurrection/Ascension Catholic Church in Rego Park, Queens. As expected for a popular pastor of a large congregation, the church was packed. Almost two hundred of his fellow priests and hundreds of his parishioners attended the mass. But also quietly participating were several Protestant ministers and laypeople. They were there because they had known Monsignor Dooley and worked with him through their congregations' mutual involvement in the Queens Citizens Organization.

Such an ecumenical experience is only a manifestation of an underlying reality that derives from the arena of action. Liturgy is not a means to understanding, it is an end.

Community organization is a place where people of differ-

ent races and religions and economic circumstances and ideologies can get to know each other as they really are—which is
the only way that a true relationship can be formed. The point
is not that people necessarily *like* those who are different from
themselves, but that they *respect* others and their values
enough to work together.

Organized religion has a terrible record for this kind of cooperation. The notion that it has a corner on the truth is a hard
one for each religious group to shake. It is difficult at times to
get religious bodies even to talk with others who disagree with
them on basic theological or moral issues—much less to develop a joint plan of action. How, they feel, can they possibly be in
the same organization with someone who believes (or doesn't
believe, as the case may be) in abortion, or aid to parochial
education, or non-violence, or women's rights or affirmative
action, or . . . the existence of God?

Here are three reasons why they should:

1. *Self-Interest.* Quite simply, there is no congregation
that can win on its own those issues that are tearing apart communities and families in this country. No national religious
group—not the Catholic Church, not the American Jewish
Committee, not the National Council of Churches, not the
Moral Majority—can win on important matters without allies.

2. *Evangelization.* Every congregation and every denomi-
nation claims that one of its primary concerns is evangelization
of the forty-one percent of adult Americans who are not members of any church or synagogue. What better place for evangelization than out in the world where the people to be saved
are struggling to survive and are crying out for help?

3. *Understanding.* History has pretty well established that
truth is not the exclusive property of any one religion. Groups
that are turned inward and do not mix it up with people of different ideas and beliefs miss the chance to learn more about
others—and themselves.

Does this mean that congregations must compromise or give up their beliefs and "get into bed" with anybody? Of course not. It just means that self-righteousness should be foregone in the name of trying to get something accomplished.

Philosopher John Herman Randall, Jr. gave an explanation of this necessity in his article "On the Importance of Being Unprincipled":

> In fact most of the world's political difficulties today focus on men's preference for laying down principles and fighting over them rather than engaging in the give and take of discussion and eventual compromise. So it seems worth-while to emphasize the importance of being unprincipled in political action. In political action, mind you—for in themselves principles are fine things. In their proper place of course they are quite indispensable. But that place is not to regulate the group activities of men. Men can live together and succeed in accomplishing things cooperatively only if they have the patience and the intelligence to compromise. It would of course sound less unconventional if instead of speaking of unprincipled action I spoke of "the principle of compromise," meaning thereby the principle of acting without regard to one's principles in the interest of acting with other men. . . .
>
> Cooperation between human beings is possible only if they are willing to compromise; and politics, the art of cooperation, of group action, is at bottom nothing but the practical application of the method of compromise. Only two kinds of men can really afford the luxury of acting always on principle: those who never act at all, who live in a sort of social vacuum, who never try to get other men to do anything; and those who have so much power they don't have to regard the wishes or habits of other men but can just give commands. . . .[26]

There are but three criteria that all groups with whom the congregation enters into alliance should be required to meet:

1. *Equality.* They must subscribe to the basic assumptions of American society that "all men are created equal, and they are endowed by their Creator with certain inalienable rights, and that among these are life, liberty and the pursuit of happiness. . . ." But they do not have to agree that busing is good (or bad), that social security payments should be raised (or lowered), or that more military aid should be given to Israel (or the PLO).

2. *Democracy.* They must believe in democracy and majority rule. Inside the organization, this is the only basis on which issues and tactics can be decided without blowing the alliance apart. On the other hand, the majority should be careful not to adopt positions that are morally offensive to part of its membership. If it does so, then the minority has no choice but to leave the alliance—often noisily—and everyone will lose the power, the chance for evangelization and the opportunity for understanding that the alliance offered in the first place. It is in the interest of all concerned to leave as much ideological baggage as possible at the door of the organization.

3. *Accountability.* They must be willing to pay their fair share of the dues, accept quotas for major actions, and accept responsibility for successes or failures. Assignments ought to be proportional and flexible among the various groups in the alliance, but they have to be taken seriously. Otherwise, the congregation finds itself in the position of compromising its principles with those who add nothing and subtract much from the power of the organization.

BLACK, WHITE, BROWN, YELLOW, RED

Almost every religious body in America spends huge amounts of time and money trying to combat racism. None of this appears to have made a huge change in the attitudes of members at the congregational level. People seem capable of hanging onto their prejudices no matter what kind of sermons, educational programs or sensitivity sessions are thrown at them.

Community organization can help. It provides a place where members of congregations can be exposed to those of other races—not in a "touchy-feely" way, but in a common effort that makes sense to all sides.

Queens, New York is the fictional home of Archie Bunker. Many whites in Queens were those who fled neighborhoods in Brooklyn and other boroughs as they began to change racially. The deterioration of those neighborhoods was blamed by many on the racial change, and so they fear any repetition in their new neighborhoods. In reality, that decline often came about more because of policies of government, banks, landlords, merchants, drug dealers and other power brokers than because of any action on the part of new residents. Yet, if you tried to convince the long-time residents of Queens of that fact, you would be categorized as a "bleeding-heart liberal."

When the Queens Citizens Organization (Q.C.O.) was formed in the mid-1970's, some churchpeople feared that it would be merely a vehicle for racist feeling in the borough. During its first years, the organization was very heavily based in the white Lutheran and Catholic parishes of Queens because major black churches, Jewish synagogues, and other Protestant denominations kept a skeptical distance.

Three things changed this situation.

First, the commitment of the organizers and leaders of the organization to broad-based diversity kept alive the invitation to membership by all segments of the Queens community.

Second, it became clear to the members of the organization that they would never have enough power if they remained as narrowly based as they were. This parochialism would be used against them by their enemies and the media labeling them a "white, Christian organization."

Third, as the organization began to win some victories, it began to attract others who were in need of allies for their own credibility and power. The historical openness of the organization to their participation allowed them to respond without embarrassment to the invitation to join.

Amazing things began to happen. Blacks and whites who had never had to deal with each other as anything other than stereotypes suddenly discovered that they had to depend on each other in the midst of battles. They also discovered that the same forces that were affecting white communities were also destroying minority neighborhoods—often more immediately and severely.

For example, the fight with the Port Authority—which involved the entire Q.C.O. organization—was initiated by a small, black Lutheran congregation in the Springfield Gardens neighborhood near JFK airport. St. Peter's had been attacked by an arsonist after it had refused to sell out to the air freight industry, and had been waging a lonely battle to save its neighborhood from the expansion of the airport for years. Through Q.C.O., St. Peter's was able to attract the allies from all over the borough that it needed. St. Peter's has now rebuilt its church and stands as a symbol of hope in its community.

By the early 1980's, Q.C.O. was one of the few working examples of a real black-white coalition in the country, with half of its member congregations and organizations black and half white. Much work is still needed to be done with other large ethnic groups in the borough, but the model for cooperation is there.

PROTESTANT, CATHOLIC, JEW

Americans of different religious persuasions are probably more open now than at any time in history to working together. Starting with the various ecumenical efforts among the Protestant and Orthodox denominations, continuing with the Catholic turnaround at Vatican II, and including overtures on both sides of the Jewish and Christian communities, there is an unprecedented opportunity for real cooperation and understanding.

This opportunity can and is being lost, however, because it

is being organized from the top down. It matters less that the Pope can meet with the archbishop of Canterbury than that a local Catholic parish is working closely with its Episcopal counterpart across the street. The American Jewish community can give brotherhood awards to a prominent Christian bishop, but if the local synagogue cannot join with the Christian congregations in the area to deal with local issues of concern to all, then what is the point?

One concrete example of cooperation on the local, congregational level will do more for interreligious understanding than all the joint services, proclamations and awards promulgated by national bodies. Community organization offers a place for that cooperation to take place.

Pastor David Benke describes the experience of his congregation with the East Brooklyn Churches (E.B.C.) community organization in his article "Practical Ecumenism: 'Rebuilding the Walls' ":

> EBC is the most deeply ecumenical enterprise I have ever known. We pray, plan, sing, study and traverse the streets together across an even dozen different denominational boundaries. Yet no one in a glass tower ever exhorted us to meet, citing the annual prayer service. No dictate from on high pulled us together. Our ecumenical mandate has been developed from within, because of our common enemies, so that we might confront them from strategic common ground.[27]

There is one caveat in this process: each group must agree to disagree—or at least to avoid certain issues.

Catholics, for example, must be willing to belong to a community organization which will not touch the issues of abortion or aid to parochial education. Protestant denominations must debate the question of women's ordination elsewhere. Jewish synagogues must see that membership in an organization that takes no position on the current situation in the Mideast is still in their interest.

This is not to say that these are not legitimate concerns, or even ones of paramount importance. It merely recognizes the fact that these are areas where the various traditions will not agree and cannot act together. To insist on their inclusion would mean to deny the very existence of the alliance.

I once had to talk some members of a fledgling organization out of bringing up before the founding convention of the organization a resolution supporting the right of teachers to strike—not because I disagreed with the resolution, nor because I thought it would lose. I knew that the resolution would win by a large majority, but that an important and sizable minority would have walked out of the convention, thereby precluding the possibility of both sides getting to understand and eventually support each other.

If five percent of issues cannot be dealt with by such an alliance, there remains a huge agenda that can be dealt with across religious and ideological lines—but only if the organization is wise enough to know what to avoid.

Who knows? After some trust relationships are built up, perhaps these religious groups can begin talking about those very basic issues that divide them.

BELIEVERS AND NON-BELIEVERS

I have a friend who is not a member of any religious congregation. He is a school teacher in an inner-city public school and a fine human being. His value system is at least as strong and well thought out as most members of religious congregations. American society is full of good people like him who are non-believers in organized religion.

My friend is genuinely offended by the idea of congregationally based community organization. He feels that it is only aimed at helping to get more power for the very institutions that he has rejected. He also feels that as an individual he is excluded from even the opportunity of building that same kind of power.

I try to answer him this way: yes, community organization

tries to strengthen the ability of a local religious institution to deal with the problems of its members and its community. It is not, however, the religious identity that is being organized, but the sociological network of people and values. My friend's "problem"—from the organizer's point of view—is not that he is not a member of a congregation, but that he is a loner. He brings no additional power to the organization and cannot be held accountable for producing either people or money to help the organization win its battles.

If he were to organize a group of people who agreed with his values—into a neighborhood club or a teachers' union or an "Agnostics Society"—then that group should and would be welcomed into any community organization on the same basis as every other group.

There are many such civic and civil rights groups, unions, business associations, senior citizen groups, and academic and health-related institutions that are prime candidates for any community organization. Congregations attempt to exclude or discourage them at the risk of lessening the power of the organization and ultimately destroying its credibility.

These non-religious groups must be evaluated for membership on the same basis of any congregation: Do they subscribe to the basic values of equality and justice, will they abide by the rules of democracy inside the organization, and can they be held accountable? If so, then they must be welcomed into the alliance or the community organization is a sham, a bogus operation that does not in fact represent the community and is rather a lobby for a particular—in this case, religious—interest group.

CLASS: POOR, WORKING, MIDDLE

Besides race and religion, economics is the other major dividing line in American society. Historically, the poor, the working class and the middle class have been pitted against each other and diverted from realizing that their interests lie more together than apart.

Let's take the issue of arson as one example.

Poor people are affected by arson most directly. It is usually their homes that are burned, their children who die. Poor people are not particularly bothered about the insurance problem caused by arson because they do not have insurance. Sometimes arson is the only way that a welfare family can get moved out of an intolerable situation by a reluctant welfare department.

Working class people are affected by arson in several ways. First, their neighborhoods are often the ones that receive the pressure to provide housing for the poor that have been burnt out of their homes. These are neighborhoods where the welfare department will pay more than the market rate for apartments, thus putting upward pressure on the rents paid by working families. Second, since the working class lives closest to the poor, their own homes are often caught up in the blight brought about by systematic arson. Consequently, they often find their neighborhoods redlined on insurance because of nearby arson. Finally, it is working class firefighters and police officers who give their lives in this battle.

The middle class suffers from arson also. Their insurance rates go up with everyone else's. Their property and income tax goes up as a combined result of a lower tax base and a need for greater fire and police service. Finally, they see the decline of their own cities and the quality of their own lives.

These three groups often find themselves pitted against one another rather than focused on the arsonists and the insurance companies and the legal system—all of which make arson one of the most profitable and least punished crimes in America.

A community organization that cuts across these class lines can do much to address itself to the root causes of issues like arson because they can avoid the temptation of blaming an easy scapegoat and can mobilize all elements of society to demand solutions. Because congregations have members from all economic levels, they provide an excellent base for this kind of alliance.

OTHER ALLIES

Potential allies for a congregationally based community organization are limited only by the imagination of the leaders and organizers. Many of these allies will never be members of the coalition, but they will provide support and advice from time to time.

Media: The media are perhaps the single most powerful ally of organized citizens. Even though the media are owned by "the establishment" and bend over backward to present that side of a story, still the media are committed to a free and open society. Individual reporters and media executives still have their own prejudices and predilections and will help a group they admire. Because the media are a profit-making venture, they can be manipulated by an organization that understands their need for action and controversy.

Politicians: Some politicians remember or can be made to recall why they got into politics in the first place. The others can be forced to do the right thing for the wrong reason. Even though the smart community organization does not endorse candidates for office, they do engage in "voter education"—which tells people how responsive a politician has been to the organization, registers the people to vote and delivers them to the polls where they can then vote their conscience.

Bureaucrats: Usually the bane of citizens who want to get things done, a few bureaucrats—usually low level ones—are more willing to blow the whistle on their superiors either because they disagree with what is going on, or they believe in power to the people, or they want to get their boss in trouble. Some of these civil servants will be members of the congregations involved in the organization and will do for it what they would never do for another group.

Intellectuals: These people are usually useless in the field of action. They are uncomfortable with the messiness of controversy and the ambiguity of most issues. They are, however, stores of knowledge and are more than willing to dispense it to anyone who asks. Usually, they give their research to the government and the corporate world, but it could just as easily be a community organization. Often these academicians have information that they would love to see people use, if only so they can study what happens with it.

Corporations: Community groups often make the mistake of lumping all corporations together. The fact is that some are truly concerned about the communities in which they operate and are willing to help in whatever ways they can. The others are very susceptible to pressure and the threat of bad publicity. Either way, corporations can be worked with by citizens' organizations to accomplish community goals. The most important thing to remember is that the self-interest of corporations is very easy to understand: the maximization of profit. Talk in those terms is sure to get an audience and a reaction.

PUBLIC AND PRIVATE

The forging and continuation of these alliances is dependent on congregations understanding the difference between people's public and private lives. Reinhold Niebuhr was very clear on the distinction in *Moral Man and Immoral Society:*

> Teachers of morals who do not see the difference between the problem of charity within the limits of an accepted social system and the problem of justice between economic groups holding uneven power within modern industrial society, have simply not faced the most obvious differences between the morals of groups and those of individuals.... The relations between groups must therefore always be predominantly political rather than ethical, that is, they will be determined by the proportion of power which each group possesses at least as much as by any rational and moral appraisal of the comparative needs and claims of each group.[28]

People's private lives revolve around the need to be liked and loved, to be generous, to be intimate. If we operate that way in our public life—which many congregations teach as desirable—then we are doomed to defeat and disappointment.

What matters in our public life is not to be liked but to be respected, to be accountable, to work out one's self-interest with those of others. It is on this basis that alliances can be made. Their primary purpose is to give all participants increased power—the ability to shape the world according to their own vision. If such alliances lead to friendship and worship, that is a wonderful—but not a necessary—by-product.

Chapter 6

CONTROVERSY: DISAGREEMENT IS NOT ALWAYS DISAGREEABLE

Do not suppose that I have come to bring peace to the earth: it is not peace I have come to bring, but a sword.
                                    Matthew 10:34

Congregations avoid community organization because they understand that of necessity it entails controversy, and controversy is the most unwanted commodity in American religious institutions. The possibility of offending anyone—either inside or outside the congregation—is compulsively avoided under the mistaken impression that people do not want to be affiliated or deal with a controversial house of worship. This premise flies in the face of the lessons learned from the history of religion. One would be hard pressed to assemble a more controversial list of characters than Jesus, Muhammed, Moses, Buddha and their followers.

Evelyn and James Whitehead make a crucial point in their book, *Community of Faith: Models and Strategies for Developing Christian Communities:*

> In our ceremonies and sermons we dwell upon images of unity and peace and joy. These images of life to-

gether as Christians are important and true, but partial. When, as a believing community, we do not speak concretely about the more ambiguous experiences of anger and frustration and misunderstanding in community life, we can leave many people confused and disappointed about their own relationships in groups.

. . . Conflict is both a normal and expected ingredient in any relationship—whether friendship or team work or family life—that brings people together and engages them at the level of their significant values and needs. . . .

Conflict is more often a sign of a group's health than it is a symptom of disease. The presence of conflict among us most often indicates that we are involved in something that we feel is significant—significant enough to generate the disturbance and tensions we are experiencing. Thus, conflict marks a relationship of some force. This energy can be harnessed. . . .

Groups in which there is nothing important enough to fight about are more likely to die than are groups in which some dissension occurs. Indifference is a greater enemy of community than conflict.[29]

Fr. James Callan was a seminary classmate of mine. Since his ordination, he has been involved in controversy of one sort or another. About six years ago, he was made the pastor of Corpus Christi parish in the inner city of Rochester, New York. Jim did not change his controversial ways, but rather celebrated them. His congregation became involved in everything from feeding the hungry each night in the basement of the church to rehabilitating the housing stock in the community; from day-care to experimental liturgies. The result was that a congregation which had less than two hundred members remaining now counts six hundred worshipers and another four hundred who regularly participate in parish programs.

In the 1960's and 1970's, many main-line congregations lost members. At the same time, many conservative congregations gained in affiliation. The assumption then and now was that congregations lost or gained members to the extent that they pushed or ignored activism. Churches and synagogues all over the country pulled back from political involvement, only to see some of those same conservatives move into the forefront of social action on such controversial issues as school prayer, abortion and military preparedness.

Is this just a simple matter of religious people being "conservative" and only objecting to the involvement of their congregation in issues that they perceive as "liberal" or "radical"? Or is it that activists misunderstood what had happened to them?

Jim Callan has this opinion: "The activism has got to spring from the congregation itself, not be superimposed by the pastor or a few lay leaders. People have got to be involved in the decisions and in the execution of those decisions. Church people have no problem with an activism that makes sense to them."

RULES FOR CONTROVERSY

There are several rules that a congregation should follow as it attempts to become involved in this type of activism.

Rule 1: *Listen.* Before beginning any program of involvement, there must be a long period of listening to the self-interest of members and potential members of the congregation. This listening can only take place in individual interviews and small group meetings where the story of the congregation is elicited and pieced together: where does the congregation come from, what are its concerns, where does it want to be, what sorts of things would its members be willing to act upon together?

Rule 2: *Count.* Be very careful of the one or two vocal (and possibly generous but usually not) members of the congregation who believe that religion is only about spirituality and the "other world." Fear of losing those people might blind the congregation to others who believe the opposite and are looking for a community of people who are committed to this world as well as the next. Many of the latter—and they are often the younger ones—are the ones who drift away from congregations or simply never join one.

Rule 3: *Capitalize.* Instead of running away from controversy, use it to build the congregation. Religious people are not very different from everybody else. They want to be where the action is. The TV preachers understand this fact, which is why it bothers them not a bit to be the center of controversy. Each time they are attacked, their membership increases and their donations rise. A controversial congregation can demand a higher level of support in both time and money than one that stands for nothing.

Rule 4: *Democratize.* If a congregation is going to act together, it must decide together what it will do, on which issues and in what manner. Then when the controversy comes—and it will come—the congregation will take it personally rather than blame the clergy or the lay leaders for getting it involved in "trouble." This does not mean that the congregation must subscribe to an immobilizing homage to consensus. Majority rule and the opportunity to have their feelings heard are enough for most reasonable members of a congregation.

Rule 5: *Be Wise.* Pick those issues and those tactics that the people in the congregation can accept. Each congregation has its own traditions, strengths and insights. If these are kept firmly in mind and built upon, the congregation will be able to handle controversy very nicely. This does not mean that there is no prophetic or teaching function for the leaders or the clergy in all this, but it does mean that they have to respect the people with whom they are working.

Following these simple guidelines will allow the congregation to bring the vast majority of its members along during a controversy. It may also attract new people to the congregation. Many people of my generation do not go to church or synagogue specifically because they do not see religion as meaningful to their struggle to live and raise a family in mod-

ern American society. Yet I have also seen people rejoin a congregation because it became involved in a community
organization effort that was actually helpful to them in dealing
with their problems and was willing to accept the controversy
entailed.

ROMANTICISTS

Saul Alinsky used to describe them as the type who walk
out of the bar the minute the argument turns into a fight.
Reinhold Niebuhr's word for them was "romanticists." He
charged that ". . . romanticists have so little understanding for
the perils in which modern society lives, and overestimate the
moral resources at the disposal of the collective human enterprise so easily, that any goal regarded as worthy of achieve-
ment by them must necessarily be beyond attainment."[30]

Romanticists exist in every congregation. They talk a lot
about the world as they would like it to be, but back away from
rolling up their sleeves and getting involved in the controversy
and conflict that any real change necessitates. They think that
somehow truth and logic, rather than power and compromise,
will alter existing institutional arrangements.

What irritates members of congregations about activism
more than anything else is when it is all talk and no action—
especially when the talk is all aimed at them as "challenges to
the laity" or "consciousness raising sessions." People can do
without this type of lecturing when it contains no specific sug-
gestions or vehicles for action. During the televised U.S. Catholic bishops' debate on their war and peace pastoral letter,
Bishop William McManus of Fort Wayne-South Bend noted
simply that religious leaders are quite specific when it comes
to telling the government what it can and cannot do, but infu-
riatingly vague when they advise their people what steps
should be taken at the congregational level.

On the other hand, when Bishop Raymond Hunthausen of
Seattle announced that he was withholding half of his personal

income tax as a protest of the arms races, there was fear that there would be a drop in donations to the diocese. The opposite happened as people showed their approval of controversial action over controversial talk by increasing their annual donations.

Another vital ingredient that good activists understand implicitly but that romanticists often miss is the value of relationships. Jim Callan understood a long time ago that people will support controversial figures a lot sooner and longer if they have a real relationship with them. Americans do not support controversial ideas, they support controversial people.

Eugene V. Debs polled almost a million votes as the Socialist candidate for president in 1920 while he was still in prison for speaking against U.S. involvement in World War I. Debs received these votes not because people believed in socialism so much as in Debs as a person. Debs had spent a lifetime crisscrossing the country, developing relationships with working people all over the country as a labor leader and a backer of radical causes. Most people voted for Debs because they felt a relationship with him, not necessarily because they agreed with his politics.[31]

My father was a veteran of World War II. He was raised in that Cardinal Spellman period of American Catholic history when the Church seemed to be an extension of the military establishment. During the Vietnam War, when first I and then my brothers came to the conclusion that we were conscientious objectors, it was at first extremely difficult for Dad—like many of his contemporaries—to accept. But primarily because he knew us and loved us, he listened and finally came to agree with that radical and controversial step. The fact that my father eventually wrote the draft board that not only was I a conscientious objector, but—by God—so was he, was a triumph of relationship over ideology.

Several years ago, Fr. Eugene Lynch, a Montfort Missionary priest and, at the time, the pastor of St. Mary Gate of Heaven parish in Ozone Park, Queens, had a celebrated confrontation with then newly elected Mayor Edward Koch.

Fr. Lynch was serving as the first president of the Queens Citizens Organization and was moderating a public meeting between the organization and the mayor. When Koch demanded a change in the agenda to make a speech, Lynch refused and Koch walked out in front of an audience of fifteen hundred—accusing Fr. Lynch of being a radical or worse. People at the meeting, the media and citizens all over New York City were split between those who blamed the mayor for being arrogant and those who blamed Fr. Lynch for being petty and unreasonable. However, Fr. Lynch's parish of five thousand middle and working class conservative families was almost unanimously in support of their pastor—not because they were used to him running a popular mayor out of a meeting, but because they had a long relationship with Fr. Lynch and trusted that he would act only with integrity.

Romanticists are always concerned about problems: those large, overwhelming concerns like poverty, hunger, peace, the environment, and the economy, which will never be solved. The kind of activism that will make sense to a congregation is one that breaks those insurmountable problems down into specific, immediate and winnable issues. But that takes time to bring people along, which romanticists are often unwilling to invest. Besides, it implies compromise and accommodation—two words not in most romantic vocabularies.

"END THE ARMS RACE/SAVE THE HUMAN RACE" said one parish bulletin announcement advertising yet another peace walk. What congregation could be against such an endeavor? But how many people showed up? It's not that people are against these kinds of efforts, it's just that over the long haul they won't expend much time or money or energy on them.

On the other hand, if those problems can be brought down to a local supermarket price-fixing scheme or a nearby toxic waste dump or the closing of a neighborhood school or a factory, then people can get excited and organized about them ... and maybe—just maybe—they will begin to see the connections between their situation and that of others.

However, the very process of localizing general concerns makes them more real and therefore controversial. To deal with them is therefore ambiguous and messy. Both sides of a local issue are easier to understand, opponents are well known, and tensions run high between friends. Romanticists like to keep things vague and therefore pure, community organization wants to make them concrete.

TACTICS

"He's convinced that if he's right on the issues, he's going to win." So an unidentified "White House man" described Reagan Budget Director David Stockman in a *Wall Street Journal* article analyzing Stockman's many tactical blunders.[32]

This country has seen many groups that seem to have felt—like Stockman—that just because they were on the "moral" side of an issue, they would win. Because they were out-organized, however, they lost. The air traffic controllers' union, the supporters of the equal rights amendment, and the pro-life movement are just three examples that come immediately to mind.

What all of these efforts have in common is that they misunderstand tactics. The purpose of tactics is to win: not to be controversial, not to show one's strength, not to embarrass the opposition, not to garner further support, not to raise consciousness or money, not to do action for its own sake—but to win.

Organizations do not have the right to lose. Organizers and leaders have no right to take their people into fights using tactics that they know—or even suspect—are not going to work. People's commitment to activism is tenuous enough without the risk of turning them off by losing. Enough battles will be lost using the most well-designed, innovative tactics without sending people to certain or near-certain defeat.

This discussion raises the age-old and insoluble problem of means and ends. Romanticists can make entire careers on this question alone. It paralyzes many groups—especially religious ones—from ever acting at all. The only possible position that one can take and still live in the world is to put the question in the only way that it can be practically answered: "Does this particular end justify this particular means?" It is not to advocate "situation ethics" to admit that moral decisions must be made in real situations.

Reporter Anne Keegan filed a story in *The Chicago Tribune* which poignantly presented one man's ethical dilemma as he considered his tactical options.[33]

It seems that Jerry Yanoff was an open-minded father who allowed his son David to go off for a month to visit his mother—who had joined a Hare Krishna temple. David got involved in the cult, and when Yanoff tried to bring him home, the Krishnas hid him.

Yanoff tried everything: publicity, the courts, letters, petitions, even attempting to carry David off (which the Krishnas physically prevented him from doing). Finally, Yanoff hit on the tactic that worked. He began to frequent the airport where the Krishnas were making thousands of dollars a day in contributions and he started to interrupt their efforts. Both Yanoff and the friends he organized kept it up for months, until finally the Krishnas were losing so much money that they offered to give David back.

There was no understanding on the part of the Krishnas. Yanoff had to sign a legal agreement not to interfere again with their solicitation at the airport. He also agreed not to speak to the media about the case or to make any more demands. Yanoff's tactics won his son back, and today David is reportedly well-adjusted. But those tactics also violated rights of free speech, religious expression and the public's right to know. Yet what parents in the same situation would not have done something similar to what Yanoff did and felt assured that they were morally justified?

Congregations involved in community organization have to make the same decisions about tactics that Jerry Yanoff had to make: Are they moral and will they be successful? The first question has to be answered inside the tradition of each congregation and based on the gravity of the issue. The second question must be answered with the following criteria in mind:

1. Tactics must have the support of a large majority of the congregation, who must see them as acceptable and necessary.
2. Tactics must be designed to cause a reaction by the opposition which will show its true nature and, in turn, help to solidify support for the organization inside the congregation.
3. Tactics must be capable of being carried out by the organization at a particular stage in its development.
4. Tactics must be able to be threatened, executed, postponed, called off or repeated as necessary.
5. Tactics must have a probability of producing victory or at least advancing the fight, and not be done merely as a symbolic protest.

If these guidelines are followed, the congregation will support the tactics. However, the kind of discipline that they imply is obviously difficult. It takes a great amount of work, lots of creativity, enough experience and often not inconsiderable luck. Here are some things to keep in mind when trying to develop winning tactics.

Surprise. The trouble with the strike as a tactic is that it is so expected in contemporary labor relations. The same goes for picketing, petitions, boycotts and letter writing for community organizations. When the auto workers first sat down on their jobs in Flint, Michigan, it was as much the element of surprise as the physical possession of the plant that won them the recognition they had sought for so long.

Humor. Most people in power cannot stand to be laughed at. Any tactic that can produce that result has a better than even chance of being successful. When the Queens Citizens Organization finally got a top official from the Port Authority to appear before two thousand of its members, it unveiled right behind the speaker's podium a huge poster of the "Port Authority Octopus" devouring Queens. This tactic completely discombobulated the official, united the audience in a good laugh, and showed up on the front page of *Newsday*.

Personalization. People cannot get upset at "the system" or "the government" or "the corporation." Some one person must be made responsible if the tactics are going to be successful. Lyndon Johnson was only one of many people who got this country into Vietnam, but it was absolutely necessary for the antiwar movement to label it "LBJ's war" if it was ever going to mobilize the mass opposition that finally got this country out of that tragic mistake.

Polarization. It is never the case that one side is completely right and the other completely wrong. But it is also true that during a conflict an organization must act as if that were true. Otherwise it would be impossible to get people sure enough of their cause to act. One need look no further than our own Declaration of Independence to observe this principle. Jefferson had no hesitation in accusing the British of every conceivable atrocity, while at the same time refusing to attribute any good to England's administration of the colonies. That was not the truth, and Jefferson and our founding fathers knew it. But they also understood that in order to get their countrymen behind their revolution and in order to win it, they had to polarize the situation. And so they did.

Accountability. When a group in Minneapolis was opposing the building of a downtown domed football stadium with taxpayers' money, the mayor announced that he would decide his position based on which way his mail went. The organization flooded the mayor's office with postcards that had been mass-produced and then held him to his promise.

Leverage. After the J.P. Stevens Company had refused for years to recognize a union, organizer Ray Rodgers dreamed up the tactic of attacking any other company which had directors on the Stevens board of directors or vice versa. Within months pressure from other companies was so great that Stevens collapsed and recognized the union.

Using these guidelines, congregations can develop tactics both acceptable to their members and capable of producing victories. Of course they will still produce controversy, but it will be the kind of controversy that builds the congregation and draws it together, rather than the kind that tears it apart.

CHURCH AND STATE

The final bugaboo for congregations on the controversy question is the problem of Church and state. No country in the history of the world has been able to achieve a clearer separation of the two than the United States. Yet sometimes it seems that the reason for the separation has been turned on its head.

The original purpose of the statement in the Bill of Rights was to prevent the state from trying to control religion or establish one religion as the state religion: "Congress shall make no law respecting an establishment of religion, or prohibiting the free exercise thereof. . . ."

Somehow, that statement—which is clearly aimed at keeping the government out of the affairs of religion—got switched to mean that religion should have nothing to say about the government. Many maintain not only that religion should not run government (which it should not), but that secular affairs are not even a proper concern of religion. This idea is contrary to the very essence of the Judaeo-Christian attitude toward the world and denies religion any real role as a teacher and promulgator of values. What is worse, it relegates congregations to a small corner of people's lives and negates the ability of the congregation to help the family cope with the many pressures tearing it apart.

As Rabbi Richard Hirsch points out in "The Jew and the City":

Many Americans cannot see why religion should concern itself with some of the problems herein discussed. They believe in morality, but confine its dimensions to personal relationship. They cannot comprehend the responsibility of the individual for society as a whole, nor the reciprocal responsibility of society for the individual. They fail to recognize the mutual dependence of human beings and their environment, and in so doing establish artificial dichotomies between the spiritual and the physical.[34]

Fortunately, most religious leaders do not buy such a perversion of the Constitution, although the misunderstanding is more prevalent at the congregational level. The U.S. Catholic bishops, in their statement *Political Responsibility: Reflections on an Election Year,* give a very clear statement of the real relationship of religion to the state—one which is echoed by similar statements by the leaders of other denominations and faiths:

> The 1971 Synod of Bishops declared that action on behalf of justice is a "constitutive dimension" of the Church's ministry and that "the Church has the right, indeed the duty, to proclaim justice on the social, national and international level, and to denounce instances of injustice, when the fundamental rights of man and his very salvation demand it." This view of the Church's ministry and mission requires it to relate positively to the political order, since social injustice and the denial of human rights can often be remedied only through governmental action. In today's world, concern for social justice and human development necessarily requires persons and organizations to participate in the political process in accordance with their own responsibilities and roles.[35]

It is understandable that the government and the existing power structure would try to sell the interpretation of the separation of Church and state that would assign religion to the spiritual realm only. But why do congregations buy it?

Two explanations are possible. One is theology. Nothing much can be said to those who buy the view of religious institutions as solely concerned with the spiritual except to point out the relatively insignificant role it assigns them in the achieving of the reign of God on earth and to suggest that they read the Scriptures more closely.

At least something can be done about the second reason, which is purely practical: congregations avoid controversy because they are afraid of losing their tax exempt status.

This concern is not unwarranted. Congregations have obligations in terms of money and buildings and programs that would make a loss of their tax exempt status disastrous and irresponsible. The argument against this concern is not—as some romanticists would have it—to degrade the tax exemption as a sellout or a constraint of the prophetic role of religion. Nor is it to advise congregations to avoid controversy.

The tax exemption is a legitimate way for society to recognize the good done by religious and charitable organizations. In addition, the power to tax churches and synagogues would also be the power to shut them up. This was one of the situations that the founding fathers were trying to avoid with the first amendment.

The argument against congregations avoiding controversy in order to protect their tax exempt status can be made on a very simple and practical level: such avoidance is neither necessary nor desirable.

It is not necessary because the law against political involvement by charitable institutions very strictly applies to—and only to—electoral politics and formal lobbying. Since community organization does neither, it is the perfect vehicle for congregational activism.

It is not desirable for congregations to avoid controversy because only when congregations are organized, willing and able to exercise power can they maintain that same tax exempt status of which they are so solicitous. Every so often there is an attempt to tax congregations in one way or another. It is only if organized religion is weak and powerless that it leaves itself open to that kind of blackmail.

So controversy is, in the end, the only path open to the congregation that wants to maintain its independence and ability to speak and act on its values. Congregations have no real choice but to learn how to handle it.

ONE STORY ABOUT CONTROVERSY

Monsignor Jack Egan, one of the true "founding fathers" of community organization in this country, once told this story about Saul Alinsky and the then Cardinal Meyer of Chicago:

Let me tell you a little story about the day that the contract was signed. It was really a handshake between Alinsky and Cardinal Meyer, who, without any strings attached, pledged $150,000 to the first three years of organizing efforts in The Woodlawn Organization. Fifty thousand a year. I was privileged to be with Cardinal Meyer in 1961 when that was done with Alinsky. As we got up to leave, Saul looked at the Cardinal, who stood about 6'6" (Saul was about 5'11"), and said, "Cardinal, when we begin this organization I hope we realize there is going to be a lot of conflict and controversy. City Hall is going to descend upon us, the whole fifth ward, the institutions of the city, a lot of elements in the black community will, and," he said, "there's going to be trouble." (This was when Woodlawn was a totally black community.) The Cardinal looked at him and said, "Mr. Alinsky, I know we do not share the same faith, but you know, no Christian should be afraid of conflict and controversy because there is nothing more controversial than a man hanging on a cross."[36]

Chapter 7

LEADERS: ARE THERE ANY VOLUNTEERS?

The reason I left you behind in Crete was for you to get everything organized there and appoint elders in every town, in the way that I told you. . . .

Titus 1:5

The final reason why American congregations do not have a serious and competent program for activism is that the leadership is spread so thin that it often ends up just running in place. By the time this distracted leadership has finished organizing the worship, maintaining the physical plant, providing social services to the needy, educating the young and pleading with members for funds, any attempts at activism are quickly relegated to the "social action" committee for prompt and ineffective disposition.

Using "good leaders" on activities "outside the congregation" is viewed as a waste of scarce resources.

To overcome this dearth of leadership, many congregations take off on a talent search for the undiscovered leaders in their midst as if they were a mineral to be mined. In so doing, the congregation puts itself in direct competition with political parties, neighborhood associations, volunteer agencies, their own denominational bodies and even people's extended families—all of which are desperately searching for the same thing: the talented volunteer.

Or, realizing that these natural leaders are not to be found, congregations spend much money hiring consultants to run high-powered leadership training courses. Many of these sessions turn out to be merely a bag of tricks that teach people some techniques of mass manipulation while leaving them totally ignorant of the true dimensions of the role of a leader.

Turn the question on its head: How should a congregation *not* go about finding and developing leaders? The answer, in most cases, is by continuing whatever is presently being done in leadership development—and proof is in the results.

What the congregation should not do is ask for volunteers. And, when it gets them (if it does), it should not expect them to be competent leaders nor expect a crash course in technique to turn them into leaders overnight.

To see how ridiculous this approach is, imagine that it was the method used by American corporations to determine their leadership:

> *Wanted:* Volunteers willing to assume the top leadership of American Conglomerate, Inc. No training or experience necessary—company will provide six-evening intensive course. No screening process, no one rejected. Must have loads of good will. Move immediately into top level of power and stay as long as you wish.

Obviously not a way to inspire investor confidence. Yet the same advertisement run in a monthly newsletter by an American congregation would seem to many not only acceptable but desirable in the spirit of equality and openness. What it would really mean, however, is that the congregation did not take itself seriously as an organization for the protection and propagation of values. No one who is serious about success turns an organization over to untried and untested leaders.

When you ask for volunteers, you are going to get one of several easily recognizable types:

1. People with lots of time and lots of psychological needs. Religious institutions are full of these people, and they should all be accepted as children of God. But that does not mean that we have to put them in charge of major elements of the life of the congregation. If you ask for volunteers, these people are going to be right there. Once you've got them, it's awfully hard to get rid of them.

2. Axe grinders. Maybe they don't like the pastor or the rabbi. Perhaps they think that TV is the instrument of the devil. Possibly they would like to be elected to the city council or state assembly. They will assume any position—no matter how unconnected to their particular concern—in order to have another forum for their economic or theological or sexual or political agenda. If you ask for volunteers, you will get them—and you deserve them.

3. "Favorites" of the clergy or the president of the congregation or the principal of the school who will do anything for their benefactor. There is no doubt that the staff will instill intense loyalty in certain people because of their position or their charisma. These subjective feelings, however, should not become the basis for building congregational leadership. If you ask for volunteers, this type is hard to avoid.

4. Burnt-out leaders who have been leading everything in the congregation for thirty years, but who always volunteer—even while complaining that "nobody else around here ever does anything." This attitude, of course, is one of the primary reasons for the fulfillment of that particular prophecy. Contin-

ue to solicit volunteers and you will continue to endure this well-meaning type, thereby stifling any new leadership that might even conceivably come forth.

5. Untrained people whom nobody else wants. Sometimes there is a gem in the rough, but usually these are immediately thrown in over their heads where they either drown or learn how to lead by a lengthy series of trials and errors. By that time, they are either "burnt-out" themselves or they are ripped-off by some other institution desperately searching for leaders. If you ask for volunteer leaders, you are going to get a pig in a poke. Sometimes you get lucky; most often it's a disaster.

In sum, congregations should follow the corollary of the old rule known by every army recruit. Never ask for volunteer leaders—not from the pulpit, not in the weekly bulletin, not in flyers, not in public meetings, not in letters, not in posters.

Instead, a congregation needs a game plan for the development of its leadership that includes three things: an idea of whom they are looking for, a method of propositioning those people and an arena in which to train them in the skills that they need.

Involvement in community organization can provide the congregation with such a plan.

FINDING LEADERS

Yahweh chose a man with a speech impediment to lead the Israelites out of Egypt. Jesus chose an uneducated, headstrong fisherman and an intellectual zealot to build his Church. None of them volunteered, nor were they obvious choices. What qualities did they have that God saw and we might not?

To make the same question more immediate and answerable, why has a woman like Lorraine Lynch become a real leader, while others in her congregation have not?

Lorraine had none of the attributes often expected and demanded in a church or community leader: she was not a good public speaker; she was not especially glamorous or educated; she did not have a lot of experience in the business or political worlds. Yet this fifty-year-old mother of five is now one of the best congregational leaders in New York City.

The answer to this transformation—according to Lorraine, her pastor and her family and friends alike—is the involvement of her parish, Our Lady of Grace Catholic Church, in the Queens Citizens Organization.

This is the parish in Howard Beach that fought for the Hallihans and their boiler in the early days of the organization. It is a blue-collar Queens neighborhood now in the shadow of the mammoth JFK International Airport. To have a conversation in Howard Beach, one must learn to stop periodically while the planes land or take off overhead.

Lorraine's husband works for one of the many air freight businesses that have sprung up all over southeast Queens around the airport. Her youngest daughter works as a groom at Aqueduct Racetrack, right at the edge of Howard Beach. Lorraine worked as a housewife and mother most of her adult life. She served as a board of elections inspector for the Republican Party, but otherwise was only mildly active in her community or her parish—and certainly not as a leader. Several years ago, when her neighbors created a huge traffic jam at Kennedy Airport to protest the planned landing of the new Concorde jet, Lorraine did not even join in. "I just never saw myself as an activist," she says.

Five years after refusing to even participate in that demonstration, Lorraine Lynch has now addressed audiences of two thousand of her fellow citizens, confronted the executive director and the board of directors of the Port Authority of New York and New Jersey which runs the airport, gone toe to toe with the governor and the mayor of New York, been interviewed by television and the *New York Times*, and helped change public policy toward the communities surrounding the airport.

In addition, she has become a valued leader in her parish, serving on the parish council, helping to head up the annual bazaar that raised $140,000, and even assisting at training sessions for her fellow parishioners.

What are the qualities that she already had—before any trainer ever met her—which allowed Lorraine to undergo that kind of growth? They are the same qualities that congregations must begin to look for in potential leaders among their own membership.

Stability. Lorraine Lynch is very clear on her values and her self-interest. As shown by her refusal to participate in the anti-Concorde demonstrations and her membership in the Republican party in very Democratic Queens County, she is skeptical of the latest fad and the prevailing wisdom. She has put a lot of time and effort into building a strong family life—something she is not about to risk for any temporary cause or activity.

Accountability. Lorraine is interested in reciprocal relationships. This is as true in her family life as in her public life. When she says she will do something, you can be sure that it will be done. She demands the same from those she deals with.

Power. Lorraine has an innate understanding of the moral neutrality of power. She believes very strongly in the values she professes and is interested in ways to make them a reality and to fight anyone who would challenge them. But she is only interested in battles she has a chance of winning. No tilting at windmills for this lady—or blocking traffic outside the airport.

Anger and Humor. On the one hand, Lorraine cares enough about what happens to her family and community to let her Irish-German blood boil. Yet she also knows enough to laugh at herself and others in what is necessarily an imperfect world. Thus, she avoids both the passivity of the too-well-tempered personality who does nothing and the consuming self-righteousness of the ideological true believer.

Patience. Lorraine has learned this virtue through thirty years of marriage to the same man and the growth to adulthood of five children. It now enables her to listen to others, to spend the time necessary to plan and reflect, to allow others to develop, to make mistakes, and to wait for the proper setting to act and react.

Vision. Leaders lead. But to do so, they must have some idea of what they would like the world to be like. Lorraine is no dreamer, but she does have ideas about what she would like to see for herself, her family, her neighborhood and her Church. While it is true that good leaders stay inside the experience of their people, it is also true that good leaders have some idea where they want to end up.

It is these and other natural, already-present qualities that congregations should be searching for in new, potential leaders. They are traits that can be observed in all of their activities and in their basic reactions to events.

The task is to get people like Lorraine Lynch to see themselves as leaders and then to give them the skills they need to perform that function for the congregation and the community. One thing is sure—they are not about to volunteer themselves.

PROPOSITIONING LEADERS

There is only one way to get new leaders with these kinds of characteristics. That is to ask them: personally, individually, one-to-one—in short, to proposition them.

Propositioning is almost a lost art in American congregations. Perhaps corrupted by television and modern advertising, Americans constantly think they can "sell" people anything. It is possible to do so for a very short time, but soon people catch on to the truth that something is not really in their interest.

Truly good salespeople quickly learn there is a much better long-term success rate when something is *pro-positioned*—put before—someone and accepted after some thought than when it is shoved down the person's throat by guilt or trickery or false promises.

Propositioning is a lot more work than selling. It also has a much higher turn-down rate. On the other hand, when it works—it sticks.

There are several elements in making a proposition that cannot be ignored:

1. A serious proposition can only be made by someone with whom there is a relationship. The nature of a proposition is that it is based on trust, since it is only as good as the person who is making it and the person to whom it is made.

2. A proposition is always reciprocal. Someone cannot be asked to do something if it is not clear what the other person is willing to do in return. Sometimes that might only mean the level of support offered the person if the proposition is accepted. Other times, it might be a strict *quid pro quo*.

3. Because it is relational and reciprocal, a proposition can only be done in an individual meeting. Any good proposition—marriage, new job, political appointment—is done this way. It implies that the matter is serious and important.

4. A proposition always lays out exactly what is being asked. No "seducing" or deceiving potential leaders. They will resent it later. It should be clear what is being asked in terms of time, money and energy. And because it is reciprocal, propositions are also negotiable. There is no such thing as a "take it or leave it" proposition.

5. Obviously, a proposition must be in the person's self-interest. Therefore, it is always able to be refused. In making the proposition, one might have made a mistake about the person's motivation. Or sometimes potential leaders do not understand how a leadership role will meet their own needs. A true proposition will respect these possibilities.

6. A proposition is also a challenge. If it holds out nothing new for the person, then there is really nothing being "put before" the person except a task already mastered.

7. For all of the above reasons, a proposition leaves a person time to consider. This is in the interest of the propositioner as well as the propositionee, because it precludes the danger of "talking them into it."

If people with the talents of a Lorraine Lynch are correctly propositioned about taking a leadership role in a congregation, there is a good chance that they will accept. And if they accept and are given the proper support and training, there is a likelihood that they will succeed.

TRAINING LEADERS

William Droel writes in his article "Confident Laity" that laypeople "must insist that the number one budget item in our parish be the provision of the best leadership training program for us laypeople."[37]

What is needed is not the Dale Carnegie course or assertiveness training that so often passes for leadership development in religious congregations. Rather, congregations need a systematic program for taking a person like Lorraine Lynch— who already has a lifetime of values and personal qualities developed—and offer her a forum for learning the skills necessary to become a leader.

Nicholas Von Hoffman, the well-known columnist and former Alinsky organizer, said it best in his paper *Finding and Making Leaders:* "Leaders are found by organizing, and leaders are developed through organization."[38]

It is precisely in the development of new leaders that the community organization comes to the direct aid of the congregation. As Von Hoffman points out:

> The kinds of leadership (the community organization) must have to operate successfully are the kinds that cannot exist in the community, because no one or almost no one in the community has the chance to gain any experience with big organizations ... they will not have had the opportunity to acquire a sense or a feel for the big organization, how it is put together, how it stays together, and what you have to do to run it. ... We are speaking of people whose organizations are mostly small and, consequently, whose leaders are schooled in the techniques which work for small groups, but seldom for large ones.[39]

The community organizing process offers people a real-world, non-academic situation in which to learn how to become leaders—especially if the organizers and leaders of that organization are committed to that development. It was several years of involvement in a serious organizing effort with its attendant successes and failures that gave Lorraine Lynch the skills that are now so valuable to her and her congregation.

Some of the skills are as mundane as how to run a meeting, how to speak in public, how to relate to the media, how to conduct interviews with fellow congregants and neighbors, and how to schedule time. Other skills are much deeper and harder to learn: how to break problems down into manageable pieces, how to create and control tension, how to negotiate, how to do strategic planning.

The fact that this training is done in and through the congregation's involvement in a community organization offers several distinct advantages to the congregation.

1. The congregation is unable to provide the number or variety of experiences for enough of its members fast enough to produce many new leaders. Community organization offers an unlimited supply of such experiences.

2. Most congregations by themselves cannot afford the services of a full-time professional organizer with the ability and the commitment to proposition and train new leaders. A broad-based community organization can offer that opportunity.

3. As most military and corporate managers know, the best place for people to develop is away from their narrow, parochial environment. Community organizations can be a multifaceted adult education university that will broaden the horizons of the congregational members who are involved.

4. By using the community organization process for training its leaders, the congregation moves the question of activism into the very center of the life of the congregation rather than leaving it on the periphery. Besides giving the congregation an efficacious and sensible vehicle for involvement in the world around it, community organization becomes vital to the

future life of the congregation itself by producing its future leaders.

The danger is that the community organization process divorces itself from the self-interest of the congregation and becomes a distraction and a drain of talent from the congregation. This destroys the purpose of congregational involvement. Congregations must therefore insure from the beginning that these newly trained leaders maintain their allegiance and roots in the congregations and are willing to use those skills for the congregation.

This safeguard lies in the very nature of the initial proposition—between the organization and the congregation and between the congregation and its potential leaders.

CONCLUSION:
UNCOMFORTABLE NECESSITY

Remember, I am sending you out like sheep among wolves; so be cunning as serpents and yet as harmless as doves.
Matthew 10:16

For many congregations of all faiths, belief in God necessitates involvement in making the world a better place. It is that simple ... and that difficult—difficult not only because it is hard and sometimes frustrating work, but also because the responsibility inherent in the task demands effectiveness as well as good will.

Community organization offers a way for American congregations to fulfill that biblical mandate in a manner consistent with their religious and civic heritage. It avoids the limitations of the approaches of direct service, individual activism, resolutions and electoral politics.

To become involved in community organization, however, congregations must address several uncomfortable questions.

—Are they willing to listen to the needs and concerns of their own people and begin organizing there, or must they demand immediate understanding and commitment to global problems?

—Can they accept the ambiguities and dangers of the pursuit and exercise of power in defense of their values and families, or will they retreat into an ethical purity that negates action?

—Will they build organizations that will be strong enough and permanent enough to negotiate with other power institutions, or will they constantly react to crises by forming movements with no structure, no money, no discipline and no accountability?

—Do they systematically seek allies of all kinds to increase their power and diversity, or do they limit themselves to those who think exactly as they do?

—Can they handle controversy and welcome it as a method of clarifying differences, or will they attempt to conciliate all arguments in a vain attempt to reach consensus between opposing value systems?

—Are they committed to the development of a growing group of serious, trained leaders capable of running both the community organization and the congregation, or will they continue to rely on well-meaning volunteers?

The answers to these questions will determine the ability of a congregation to participate in this type of activism. The necessity of such activism lies in what it can do for the congregations themselves.

1. Congregations can begin to serve as a mediating institution between their members and the larger society. No longer will the congregation be seen merely as a place of sabbath worship with no connection to the daily concerns of its people. Rather, it will become a place to which people turn for help in solving their problems of attempting to live a religious life in a society that mocks those values.

2. Congregations can cease being merely hospitals that dispense bandages to the physically and psychologically wounded. Instead of bemoaning the disintegration of the family or the destruction of the neighborhood, congregations can begin to address the root causes of those problems.

3. Congregations will have a training ground for the next generation of leadership. These new leaders will be tested in a

variety of situations and will develop the skills needed to run the congregation: power analysis, strategic planning, recruitment, fund raising, issue analysis, mobilization of resources.

4. Congregations will have a place to meet people of different faiths and even no faith in an atmosphere of cooperation and acceptance. There will be a real reason for being together and a real chance for understanding.

5. Congregations will gain the respect of those in power as they become more sophisticated and less able to be manipulated. They will begin to be included among the interest groups who determine the American democratic consensus.

6. Congregations will begin winning concrete victories that help to stabilize their community and their own membership. These victories will be negotiated compromises with other power institutions and they will have a specific material as well as symbolic value.

7. Congregations will begin to involve their people on immediate, local issues that will convince their members of the need and religious justification for activism. That involvement will lay the groundwork for teaching the connections between local examples of injustice and national and international concerns.

8. Congregations will become exciting and determining institutions in the community that will draw people—especially young people—into membership. This form of evangelization may well succeed where many others have failed.

9. Congregations that are more involved in the lives of their people will see their contributions rise as members perceive the congregation as being concerned about their needs. This increased stewardship will more than offset any resources the congregation spends on its involvement in the community organization effort or losses from disgruntled members opposed to any form of religious activism.

10. Congregations will develop a more competent laity that will be able to turn its talents to the running of the congregation itself. Community organization is basically a lay activity—even though it needs the blessing and involvement of the clergy. The experience and the self-confidence developed

by the laity in this process can be well used by a congregation whose clergy welcomes that participation.

Every community organization is not going to produce all of these benefits for every congregation. Some efforts will fail; others might even have negative effects. The potential, however, is there, and any risks are well worth taking for congregations looking for an activism that makes sense.

APPENDICES

Appendix I

THE BIBLICAL IMPERATIVE: A STATEMENT BY THE CLERGY OF THE QUEENS CITIZENS ORGANIZATION(Q.C.O.)

1981. Used by Permission of the Queens Citizens Organization, 87–04 88th Avenue Woodhaven, N.Y. 11421

FOREWORDS

I am deeply grateful to those who collaborated in the writing and production of: "The Biblical Imperative." It is a clear expression of the Judaeo-Christian tradition that forms the basis of the Queens Citizens Organization.

It has been most gratifying to watch the growth of Q.C.O. over the past four years. I am impressed with the relationships that have developed during this period. Clergy and laity, working together, have shown what skillful leadership can effect.

We thank Almighty God for the inspiration and courage that he gives to our generous brothers and sisters who are committed to protecting the dignity of each person, the growth of community, and the development of viable and family oriented neighborhoods. Q.C.O. shares its talents for the good of our city.

I urge all our parishes to join in this needed and important ecumenical effort. May Almighty God continue to bless all the endeavors of Q.C.O.

Francis J. Mugavero, Bishop
Diocese of Brooklyn and Queens
(Roman Catholic Church)

"We do claim vigorously the right to introduce our values into public dialogue." That brief sentence from "The Biblical Imperative" of the Queens Citizens Organization sets forth the redemptive mission of religious persons in the world. The religious values which we all cherish need more than to be proclaimed. If those values are to mean anything in our society they need to be lived out in the arenas of law and politics and economics. The converse is to say that if these values are not worth fighting for why hold them as valuable.

The Queens Citizens Organization provides a vehicle for men and women of faith to struggle against those forces in our society which do not respect those values which we cherish. It is high time that people put words into action! I am pleased to read that "The Biblical Imperative" is set forth as the foundation for this action.

James A. Graefe, Bishop
Metropolitan New York Synod
(Lutheran Church in America)

INTRODUCTION: WHAT WE BELIEVE

As men and women of biblical faith, we hold certain beliefs to be beyond debate. They are the very basis upon which we raise our families and organize our congregations. Because some do not share those beliefs, it is useful at times to name them and to hold them up to the scrutiny of ourselves and of others.

We believe that God rules in the created order and in redemptive history, that God's intention is one of justice and equity. We, therefore, do not believe that our faith requires us to withdraw from engagement in the world or to concentrate on our personal salvation while the created order goes to "hell." God calls us to be active for the life of this world and this city. This we understand to be the "biblical imperative."

To help "bring order out of chaos," it is not necessary for our local congregations to assume a position on every major issue that faces society. Many churches and synagogues have trivialized their witness in this way. Our families and congregations are "activists" in that we are doers; we are not "activists" in that we do not attempt to cover the waterfront—even of the issues that confront us. We realize that it is as important to succeed in our efforts as it is to have good intentions. Thus, we begin by seeking specific winnable victories and organize ourselves to improve actual conditions.

We organize on the basis of self-interest, which we understand to be the pursuit of our own needs in relationship with those of others. We believe that properly understood self-love and self-respect are fundamental to love of others—as opposed to selfishness which precludes others and ultimately destroys ourselves.

We believe that poor and middle-class families have valid and complementary self-interests and that alliances can be made between them on the basis of shared concerns as well as shared ideology.

We believe that the authentic self-interests of whites, blacks, Hispanics, Asians and other groups coincide to such a degree that mutual cooperation is not only desirable but necessary.

We believe that effective coalitions can be created among Christians, between Christians and those of other faiths, and between religious and non-religious institutions. We respect different theological traditions and we value theological dialogue as well as coalition-building.

Surely our interests do not divide on economics, racial or religious lines, and we resist any tendency to so divide them.

While we share many of the concerns about the pressures breaking up the family, radical change in culture brought about for fun and profit, and the shifts in acceptable public behavior, we do not believe that there are simple legislative answers to these pressures. We do not believe that change is bad of itself. Nor do we seek a religious empire or religious domination. But we do claim vigorously the right to introduce our values into public dialogue.

We are realistic about politicians, bureaucracies and human nature, but we refrain from blanket condemnations and self-defeating negativism as we seek to work through the economic and political structures we confront.

WHY WE BELIEVE AS WE DO

In the Book of Genesis it is written that people are made to the image and likeness of God and given stewardship over the things of the earth. This fundamental biblical imperative is the basis upon which our families, communities and congregations organize for power.

We can say that the whole story of Scripture is the story of redemption: of God's and God's people's unceasing struggle to see to it that human beings—all human beings—have the possibility of living in an environment which allows them to live with the dignity given to them by their Creator. With this God-given right there go the responsibilities of stewardship: for the goods of the earth are meant for the good of all, not the advantage of the few.

Refusal of these rights and denials of this responsibility are inimical to the design of the Creator and the mission of our families and congregations.

A central event of the people of God was the exodus. This experience was not a mere geographical transplantation. It was the acquisition of a freedom from an oppressive economic, social, military and religious serfdom where human rights were spurned and power exercised with wanton irresponsibility.

Much of the words, energies and lives of the prophets were directed against those forces—religious, social and military—which were trying to suppress and oppress family and congregational life. They saw their role as agitating and challenging Israel to abandon their sinful ways in order to organize themselves to create a society of justice and equity as an example to all nations.

The mission of the prophets was continued and enhanced by the life and words of Jesus. He used the words of Isaiah to summarize his work:

> The Spirit of the Lord is upon me,
> because he has anointed me to preach good news to the
>   poor.
> He has sent me to proclaim release to the captives
> and recovering of sight to the blind,
> to set at liberty those who are oppressed,
> to proclaim the acceptable year of the Lord.

Jesus' commandment to love our neighbor demands that we go beyond the effects of injustice experienced in the lives of individuals and seek out the causes embodied in those structures and institutions of economy, society and politics which perpetuate human misery. This requires our families and congregations to be engaged in the civic and political order since this is the arena in which social injustice and the denial of human rights can be remedied.

It is within the family and congregation—the core units of our society—that one discovers that if life is not created and sustained by the spiritually mature, then society will be eroded by the spiritually deformed and degenerate.

However, this involvement in the secular order must honor that sophistication required in addressing issues which are nearly always complex. It must be comprehensive and consistent and competent—as well as faithful. Otherwise, it will fail and, if it fails, will lead to victory by the forces of hatred and injustice.

Far from imperiling the political process and genuine pluralism, this involvement by our families and congregations is rather an affirmation of their importance. Nor would our activity be seen as inhibiting a free and open society. For we are aware that specific programs or specific solutions to problems are not revealed to us and that our human dignity means that God has accorded us the freedom to apply our considered opinion and choice to our decisions. This consideration precludes any religious community from forming a single-issue voting bloc.

In summary, our families and congregations, drawing on the word and examples of the Bible, must involve themselves in the process of history, must dedicate themselves to the promotion of conditions which favor human dignity, and must develop the power to effectively accomplish that goal.

The task is immense and unceasing. For, in the words of Pope John Paul II, "humanity's situation in the modern world seems indeed to be far removed from the objective demands of the moral order, from the requirements of justice, and even more of social love. . . . We have before us great drama that can leave nobody indifferent."

HOW OUR BELIEFS ARE BEING CHALLENGED

As a borough of New York City, Queens is often described as a series of "neighborhood pockets"—parochially isolated and often opposed to each other.

Our borough is composed of churches, synagogues, businesses, schools, parks, bars, restaurants, airports and racetracks. It is also the dwelling place for those families who help constitute the work force of this great city. Within these "neighborhood pockets" the core values of our families and congregations are born and sustained.

However, it is often outside and off-stage of these "neighborhood pockets" that the concrete decisions that affect the lives of our people are made and implemented—not for the families and congregations of Queens and on our value system, but for the self-interest of others who are miles away and often operate with another value system.

The invisible power of these outside decision makers is not invincible. An inherent feeling of powerlessness is being set aside as more and more people of Queens are recognizing that the values of their family and neighborhood and congregation are the crucial measurement that must be met for ascertaining the strength or weakness of any proposed measure.

The oppression of the families and congregations of Queens is a litany of calloused planning and unchecked implementation:

deterioration of city services, arbitrary taxation, transportation nightmares, failed schools, increased crime, overcrowded and broken highways, flooding and backed-up sewers, abandoned buildings and unchecked drug culture.

Two issues are exemplicative:

Arson: New Yorkers have watched with horror as whole sections of the Bronx and Brooklyn have fallen to the arsonist's torch. Yet nothing has been done to make the changes necessary in state legislation, fire prevention, prosecution and insurance policy to make arson more difficult and less profitable. As Queens residents began to realize that their borough is the logical "next" target, they discovered that neither public nor private officials had developed an effective anti-arson program for Queens.

JFK Airport: JFK Airport is the largest single employer in Queens. Moreover, it holds the greatest potential for expanded economic activity of any single facility in the city. Queens residents were shocked to discover that plans for the doubling of activity at JFK within the next ten years were being made without any consultation with the residential community surrounding it. The Port Authority of New York and New Jersey which operates JFK as a highly profitable enterprise under long term lease from the city of New York views itself as an "island" with no responsibility for the problems it causes in the surrounding Queens community. The city, state, and borough governments appear ready to write a blank check to industry to do whatever it desires to create jobs and taxes and apparently view Southeast Queens as a prime candidate for "planned shrinkage" of existing residential communities.

Little attention is given by government or industry to Queens as a place where the various cultures of our people can come alive and be shared with one another. Rather they follow a policy which pits middle class against poor, race against race, neighborhood against neighborhood, and religion against religion. The consequences of such a plan are all too clear: congregations fold, neighborhoods die, families break up or flee.

Queens people do not want to be pitted against each other any longer. They simply want to survive: worship God, maintain their security, enjoy life, raise their children, and sustain their values. Crucial to their hope of success is the involvement of their religious institutions.

Our congregations must reclaim and implement the power God has given us. This power seeks to persuade us that the Kingdom of God is not a location, but the careful working of a people who with their God change the order of things. No longer must we allow the secular powers to define our tasks because such have paralyzed our public actions on behalf of our families and congregations. There must be modern day "miracles." We must not be led astray by those inside and outside religion who wish to limit miracles to the breaking of the laws of nature. Rather, we must see miracles as the breaking of the powers of the corrupt by the presence of God's grace and activity that will transform the lives and structures of our neighborhood, borough and city.

God's power is not a power that destroys others but is a power that will cause tension as it intentionally works to unmask the "principalities and powers" of our city and borough that instead of serving the needs of people as God ordered them to do they sap the dignity of a people that God so earnestly loves.

Traditionally, Queens churches and congregations have been the agencies of our borough that have serviced and chaplained those persons and families most hurt and destroyed by those idols. However, we must do more than advocacy and direct assistance for those already injured. Our task is to take the lead in bringing the hitherto isolated "neighborhood pockets" together to get enough power to address those who would destroy our values and beliefs.

OUR RESPONSE: THE QUEENS CITIZENS ORGANIZATION

In order to act on our beliefs, to get the power that we need to build the kind of society that we value in Queens, we needed a vehicle. The isolated family, the single congregation, even the individual neighborhood could never get the kind of attention necessary to deal with the problems facing Queens. Therefore, four years ago, five congregations from five different Queens communities started the Queens Citizens Organization with their own money and money and personnel from the national Industrial Areas Foundation. It has since grown to be an organization of some thirty congregations and civic organizations representing tens of thousands of families in Queens, raising its own budget of $125,000 per year, and enjoying the full support of many denominational leaders, businessmen, union leaders, government officials and educators.

In the past, religious leaders—both clergy and laity—have tried to exercise influence through individual contacts. Often they used the "pull" that they imagined their position to have in attempting to effect change. Various groupings of religious leaders or institutions were formed to take advocacy positions on a variety of issues.

The Queens Citizens Organization takes a different approach by organizing religious congregations into an organization that attempts to mobilize its latent power to become a real part of the decision-making process. It does not pass resolutions; it mobilizes its people. It does not give "advice"; it negotiates for its members.

Q.C.O. is organized by congregations as a vehicle for the natural extension of their mission in society. The biblical values of these religious institutions are integral to the basic philosophy of the organization. Yet the membership in Q.C.O. is open to all religions, welcoming their diversity since we are convinced that there are more elements which unite us than divide us.

Q.C.O. also allows non-religious organizations which share our ideals and policies to become members since we believe that such pluralism is strength.

Ownership of Q.C.O. is jealously guarded in the sense that we are adamant in preserving our independence from any individual or group which might seek to manipulate us, either by political pressure or by financial obligations. For the same reason, Q.C.O. does not support any political party or candidate, but strives to work with officials in any capacity in promoting its goals.

To achieve these goals, Q.C.O. hires a competent staff of trained professionals to provide us with the leadership training and organizing skills necessary to be successful. Both clergy and laity are trained in how to mobilize our congregations on both internal and external matters. People are taught how to research issues and then present them effectively. They learn accurate power analysis and how to develop working relationships of accountability with public and private officials. These are skills that our families and congregations must have if they are to make Queens the best possible place to live and raise their children.

The Queens Citizens Organization is a reality. It is not going away; it has proved its value. It provides a viable means for congregations seeking to fulfill the biblical imperative. We call on those in Queens searching for such an opportunity to join us.

Appendix II

ELICITING A COMMUNITY'S STORY: THE PARISH INTERVIEW PROCESS

William M. Droel

Over and over we hear in our parish circles the same complaint: "It's always the same old people" or "We have a dearth of leadership" or "People don't participate the way they used to" or "The people out there are apathetic."

Yet at the same time we know that America is a nation of volunteers. Americans of all philosophical and political persuasions are committed to our nation's unique degree of voluntary action. The last decade witnessed a tremendous growth in the number of people forming and joining groups of all kinds: everything from Divorced Catholics to United Non-Smokers. There are over one million identifiable voluntary organizations in this country. All public policy is formulated with the presumption that this pluralism will only continue to grow. Our economy is growing more and more dependent on this thirty-seven million member "third sector." Were all the Can-

This article appeared in *Service* #3 (July/August/September), 1982, Volume 9. Used by permission of Paulist Press, 545 Island Rd, Ramsey, N.J. 07446.

dystripers and Senioraides to be salaried, they would receive $34 billion per annum.

Why then aren't all these people coming to us? Why is our parish council full of vacancies? Why is our Holy Name Society getting crusty? Why is our parish youth group faltering? Why is our K of C having another membership drive?

For the most part, the problem stems from a few basic organizational misunderstandings. In the case of a few parishes it stems from an inverted theological concept and practice.

CORRECT ORGANIZATIONAL AND THEOLOGICAL UNDERSTANDINGS: LEADERSHIP AND COMMUNITY

The columnist, Nick Von Hoffman, perceptively asserted some years ago that leaders are found by organizing. It seems simple enough, but many church and civic groups act as if leadership preceded or transcended organization.

In reaction to cries about a dearth of leadership, these mistaken groups act as if leaders were born rather than made through organizing. They begin a great hunt for new members, natural leaders, energetic workers. They assume that one more direct mailing will yield several natural leaders who will then become so interested in the pre-set program that the parish will be saved. They think, Von Hoffman writes, that they can find "the indigenous leader, the great organizational nugget, whom we will find by panning for him if we only knew what the hell he looked like and how he differed from all the silt washed into our tin."[40]

Our parishes would be miles ahead if they would give up their complaining and quit their panning and start some elemental organizing.

The formula, "Leaders are found by organizing," can be extended to read, "Communities are created by organizing." Here too we sometimes act as if some magical community preceded our organizational efforts. It is like the rector of a seminary telling the incoming class, "What we have here is community, if you aren't willing to put time into it, maybe you don't belong." Our churches have lost a lot of young people over the past twenty years. Maybe it is because too many of us thought we had an *a priori* community and that those who didn't get involved didn't belong. Sometimes we act as if it is our good news that is being promoted in the community rather than God's good news. We act out what Woody Allen only suspects: that God is an underachiever. We can never forget Pope Pius XII's paraphrase of Jesus, "The Church was made for men; men were not made for the Church."

A parish on the north side of Chicago recently had an all-day meeting of its top leadership. The topic for the meeting, however, was a contradiction in terms: "Ways To Preserve Our Parish." According to the good news, you cannot save a parish but only give it away.

An emotional and intellectual crisis occurs when we come to realize that Christianity is something to be given away and that the Church is instituted not to preserve those within it, but to save in the service all humanity. Such a crisis can be growth-promoting or it can cause those who fear reality to fill their lives up with a myriad of "saving" activities. Membership in the Church saves people only when they accept a new and more profound responsibility. As the theologian Juan Luis Segundo writes:

> The primary preoccupation of the Church is not to be directed toward its own inner life but toward people outside. The Church is not founded for the benefit of its own members but as a sign to those who live, act, and work outside the narrow limits of the Church. The Church today has too often turned itself inside out. Its primary function seems to be maintaining the mass of professed Christians within the Church, servicing their needs. Missionary action, concern for non-Christians, witness, sign bearing all get secondary consideration—if there is time, energy, and money left after all the services.[41]

The writer is saying nothing different from Jesus, who said, "He who would find his life must give it away."

A parish, a community, a Church is not what you set out to preserve but is what you get after you organize, after you missionize, after you teach, after you interview. In the process of organizing community, in interviewing for new leaders, and in inviting them to tell their stories, you may also discover that you have organized an invitation to your salvation.

A SUGGESTION FOR BUILDING PARISH: INTERVIEWING

It is amazing how many well-designed parish renewal, revival, or reform programs make home visiting a low priority or a concluding step in their schema. It is as if we think that style supersedes content in God's opinion. A well-designed and packaged program will compensate for the lack of hard missionary work, we assume. Countless meetings of several committees take the place of bringing the good news to individual homes.

From a careful study of St Paul's missionary method we learn that there is one Kingdom-building program: home visitation. Interviewing is the modern term for the same discipline. The great missionary pastors who organized the first ethnic parishes in this country knew implicitly the importance of interviewing. Today's pastors sometimes think that the method is counseling, or workshops, or mime, or values clarification. Modern missionaries could do no better than conduct forty interviews each week for the Kingdom. (These interviews could, of course, include the pastor's hospital, jail and nursing home visits.)

The successful interviewer ("inviter," "organizer," "missionary," "teacher" are synonyms) needs to be accomplished in two arts: listening and creating community. Actually these two talents are also synonymous.

Interviewers would have no trouble making the offer they can't refuse, if they could learn to be patient, sensitive, and attentive enough to hear the words and needs the community is trying to express. But because our lives are filled with the noise of a style that supersedes content, we are deaf to the Word being announced. The successful interviewer has to be quiet enough so that he or she can elicit the story of the community. We must learn to listen.

What we may be fortunate enough to hear is the story of the community. Asking for that story is in reality more precious and demanding than asking for more money in the collection or help in setting up bingo chairs. By inviting people to make the big sacrifice of sharing their story, we will get, as the British convert Douglas Hyde says, "an heroic response, and the relatively smaller sacrifices will come quite naturally."[42]

At all times we must remember that the response to our call is as free as the voluntary decision Abraham made to answer his God or as the choice anyone makes to join the United Non-Smokers. In Oakland recently the historian David O'Brien attributed the disparity between the Church's hopes and its accomplishments to a failure to take the voluntary aspect of Church affiliation seriously. The American Catholic Church (unlike its European counterpart) has always been a voluntary association.

> One reason for the fact that results have not matched hopes is the continuing inability to appreciate the fact that religious affiliation is truly voluntary. There are groups of religious professionals who are receptive to new ideas and eager to organize new programs of mission. These elites, however, often seem to think they can win mass Catholic support simply by the quality of their ideas or the moral power of their prescriptions. They forget that the Church must persuade rather than coerce, invite rather than demand.[43]

A voluntary community is an intermediate social group. It is not strictly a family nor is it a bureaucracy. Some parishes do not attract new leaders because they are run like closed clans and others are unattractive because they are run like a big business. A community is somewhere in between.

As a voluntary community of the intermediate range, a parish has to try to be both attentive to the needs of its members and at the same time concerned about its social influence. That is, it must try to convey an interior life of belonging to those new leaders it is inviting, while challenging them to work toward an exterior goal.

The interviewee has two needs: the need to be uniquely appreciated and the need to make a difference in the world.

A growing parish must invite new leaders individually, yet also impress them with the parish sense of mission or purpose. It is the common values and the vision toward the Kingdom that we share that moves us to do something more.

People who are trying to save their parish by holding on forget that mission or purpose is the essential reason why anyone joins a community. A famous professor at Harvard Divinity, James Luther Adams, put it this way several years ago:

> Voluntarism is an associational institutional concept. It refers to a principal way in which the individual through associations with others "gets a piece of the action." In its actual articulation it involves an exercise of power through organization. It is the means whereby the individual participates in the process of making social decisions.[44]

Any parish that can convey to new leaders that it is about something more than itself is going to have successful interviews in an era where the conviction dominates that there really is very little we can do about the direction of our public lives.

The interviewer must listen for these two needs—the need to belong and the need to influence—as he or she elicits the story of the community.

An interviewer who has ears to hear beneath the stale rhetoric, beyond the fears, the rationalizations, the intellectualizations, and the reactions shouldn't be surprised if he or she in one word or another gets this story:

> The second wave of industrial progress is not solving all my problems. My material deposits leave me with empty feelings. I would like to understand why I earn more and it buys less; why the young resort to drugs; why terrorists shoot presidents, popes, and poets and call it acceptable politics.

> I lack for some meaning and I hunger for value. I have a need for community. I want to associate with others like me and I want to know that others care for me. I want to grow and understand more about myself and the world in which I negotiate. I would like to influence some part of that world for the better. I am overwhelmed enough to know I can't do it alone and hopeful enough to risk doing it with you.

HOW TO RUN A MEETING

Despite the best of intentions, most organizations break down or at best limp along because they lack one simple skill: how to run a meeting.

Nor is it merely a failure to use *Robert's Rules of Order*. Too many esoteric rules cause people to throw up their hands in disgust or despair somewhere between "moving the previous question" and "calling for a division of the house." Parliamentary procedure is too often used by some hot-shots to confuse everybody else in a vain attempt to show how smart they are.

There are, however, simple, basic, common sense principles that anyone can learn and that are necessary to run any meeting.

1. *Hold a meeting only to ratify decisions that the organization is seriously expected to act upon.*

People are too busy, have too many other demands on their time to go to unnecessary meetings. Ask attendance only when it is needed—when a real decision is going to be made, when a commitment on the part of the membership to carry out the action is needed. Sharp, talented people just stop coming to meetings where "nothing happens," and the organization is left tending to the psychological needs of people with nothing better to do.

Regular monthly meetings? Quarterly meetings? Annual meetings? Cancel them if there is no action to ratify, no decision to make.

Minutes? Financial reports? Committee reports? Put them in writing and drop them in the mail.

Discussion? Brainstorming? Planning? Bull sessions? Do it informally: on the phone, at the tavern, over coffee, after religious services.

Do anything but hold a meeting with no real reason.

This will require more work ahead of time for the leaders. They must decide whether each individual meeting is worth people's time and they must plan and discuss which action proposals are to be presented well ahead of time. Members have the right to know why they have been asked to attend another meeting.

One final point: if you find that your organization never has an action to ratify, ask yourself why the organization exists. Maybe it's time to give it a decent burial.

2. *Start all meetings exactly on time and end them exactly on time.*

Most people get to religious services, movies, plays, ballgames and TV shows on time for one reason: the virtual certainty that they will start on time. Many of those same people come to meetings late because of the opposite certainty that they will start late and run long.

Those who hate to waste their time come when they think the meeting will actually start. Others wait for them before beginning. The meetings therefore in fact begin late. Those who were on time feel punished and next time join those who come late. Meetings become progressively later in getting started and therefore later in ending.

But, the leaders say, how can we start meeting without enough people or—horror of horrors—without a quorum? The answer is to just do it once or twice. The problem will clear up immediately. People tend to be embarrassed by walking into meetings that have already started. If that doesn't work, try putting the most important item first on the agenda and present the latecomers with a couple of *faits accomplis.*

Ending on time and at a reasonable hour is equally important to starting on time. If you cannot accomplish your business in one and a half hours (at most), then you need another meeting. After an hour and a half, nothing much positive gets accomplished anyway. Lots of bad things happen, however: people get testy, unwise motions get passed, people get home at midnight, their spouses suspect the worst or resent the organization, they are tired at work all the next day, and . . . they are much less inclined to attend your next meeting.

But—what if there are still important items to decide? What if debate goes on longer than expected? What if people bring up additional items? What if . . . ?

Simple. A timed, written agenda with all the proposals for action is mailed ten days before the meeting. That agenda is all that can be dealt with at that particular meeting:

SAVE THE WHALES CLUB
Star of the Sea Auditorium
95th St. and Tundra Avenue
February 30, 1984

8:00 P.M. Call to Order
Adopt Minutes (mailed with agenda; never read aloud)
Approve Agenda

8:05 P.M. President's Report

8:10 P.M. Action Proposal Number 1
Discussion
Vote

8:30 P.M. Action Proposal Number 2
Discussion
Vote

9:00 P.M. Action Proposal Number 3
Discussion
Vote

9:25 P.M. Open Discussion

9:30 P.M. Adjournment

When the allotted time for debate on one particular item is over, cut the talk—call the question, make a decision, vote! The same points are probably being made over and over again. Some use debate to wear others down rather than convince them—and that's not democracy.

This is the bottom line: get that meeting over on time so that people will want to come back. (It is, after all, the only way you can hold another meeting.)

What about the bright idea that comes to some genius during the meeting, that takes twenty minutes to deal with, and that is usually a bad idea upon reflection? For this occurrence—which happens at least once every meeting—a wonderful little device has been invented called "Open Discussion."

"Open Discussion" is a five minute item at the end of every agenda—when everyone is itching to go home—during which members are free to bring up their insights, questions and ideas on any subject for the edification of the group. Under no circumstances are these ideas voted upon then. They are aired, discussed and then referred somewhere else. If they are such great ideas they will await the next meeting when they can be presented in the form of written action proposals that have been mailed to everyone before the meeting, thought about and discussed ahead of time, and voted on after sufficient reflection. If they are not such great ideas, they can be quietly and mercifully forgotten.

3. *Use "Simplified Rules of Order."*

Robert's Rules of Order covers every conceivable situation for every possible type of meeting and is therefore too complex for anyone but experts. Therefore, this source is used by those experts not to expedite meetings but to control them.

To run the kind of normal, friendly meetings in which most congregations and community organizations are involved, it is only necessary for everyone to understand "Simplified Rules of Order," as follows.

1. Every action proposal must be made as a main motion. Only three things can then happen to this main motion. (a) It can be amended. (Each proposed amendment is dealt with as it comes up, is voted either up or down by a majority of those present and voting, and then the main motion—as amended or not—is dealt with.) (b) It can be tabled. (If there is not enough information or more time is needed or for whatever reason, the main motion can be tabled by a majority vote. If tabled, the main motion cannot be brought up again at that meeting.) (c) It can be adopted or rejected by a majority vote. (Once an issue is decided, the chairperson moves immediately to the next item on the agenda. No more discussion!)

2. After enough debate has taken place on an item, anyone—including the chair—can "call the question"—i.e., end debate and proceed immediately to a vote. (a) Informally. (The chairperson asks if there is any objection and, if none, proceeds immediately to a vote.) (b) Formally. (If there is an objection to ending debate, an immediate vote is taken. If two-thirds of those present and voting want to end debate, then the chairperson proceeds immediately to a vote. If not, then debate continues until someone else "calls the question" and this procedure is repeated.)

3. Any other question is decided by the chair on the basis of *common sense*. If anyone objects, he can "challenge the ruling of the chair." Each person—including the chairperson—can speak once on this motion for one minute at most. Then debate is stopped and a vote is taken immediately to either uphold or reject the decision of the chair. This situation hardly ever arises, but this one rule eliminates the need for hundreds of other rules of parliamentary procedure. If your chairperson

cannot rule on the basis of common sense, then get somebody else instead of making more rules.

And that's it: all you need to know to run a good and productive meeting. Will they be perfect meetings right away and every time? No. This is a public skill that—like all skills—must be learned and practiced.

The payoff for following this system is that people will leave your meetings in a reasonable amount of time and feeling that they accomplished something. That is all most people ask of any organization.

ON PROFESSIONAL ORGANIZERS

People who organize are in constant danger of creating small kingdoms for themselves. It is extremely difficult to take initiatives and develop new plans without claiming it as something that is yours.

Henri J.M. Nouwen[45]

Serious, congregationally based community organization cannot begin to reach its potential without help from experienced professional organizers.

Would that it were not so. Would that indigenous leaders could rise up, recognize their need, train themselves, form alliances with like-minded institutions, build an organization, address issues, fight and win, attract and train new leaders and then take all of their skills back into their congregation. Would that clergy had the competence and the time to interview hundreds of people, identify their self-interest, research their problems, strategize some solutions, and mobilize their people. It's not going to happen.

Saul Alinsky often commented that the organizer is a "tacit insult" to those being organized. This is true in much the same way that a missionary is a subtle or not-so-subtle putdown of the people being served. Neither would even be around if the community had been able to see the truth on its own and organized to do something about it. Here comes an "outsider"—someone not familiar with local history and customs—trying to build a new church or organization, spending full-time on the task, and expecting to be paid for the effort.

In his insightful analysis *Missionary Methods: St. Paul's or Ours?* Roland Allen gives a wonderful contrast between two well-meaning missionaries.[46]

The first missionary sought to protect his fledgling converts from the dangers of too much responsibility—lest they should be overwhelmed and lost. He worked unceasingly to raise money from the wealthy Christians in other countries so that he might provide the best possible services to his people. He was the charismatic leader who prevented his inexperienced flock from making many dangerous mistakes, either moral or theological or financial.

The second was loath to accept outside money for his work. He forced his people to found church councils and then made the councils responsible for all decisions—both major and minor. They had to raise their own money and spend it on what they thought they needed. He even let them figure out how to discipline their own members. They made many mistakes, but they learned from those mistakes.

Both missionaries eventually moved on to other assignments, as they all must do. The second left a strong local church, the first a weak dependent one. In short, argues Allen, the second used the methods employed by St. Paul in his short but unequaled history as the most successful missionary in the history of the world. The first used the method too often unsuccessfully employed by modern missionaries.

The good community organizer—and the only kind that a congregation which takes itself seriously should be involved with—is one who understands and employs St. Paul's method.

There are many of the first type of organizer around—on government or church or foundation or union payrolls. But there are only a few of the St. Paul school, and they tend to be people with considerable life experience, clarity about their own self-interest and worth, and a commitment to professionalism.

THE ORGANIZER AS AGITATOR

Organizers provoke several bad raps, which upon inspection are not necessarily negative qualities at all, but which are often used as a secret code to discredit their work.

One such charge is that they are agitators. Of course they are. An agitator, according to Webster, is "one who tries to arouse or produce dissatisfaction so as to produce changes."

Organizers not trying to produce change are simply not doing the job for which they were hired. No one employs an organizer to maintain the status quo. The real objection to what an organizer does is the "arousal of dissatisfaction"— what Alinksy called "rubbing raw the sores of discontent."

There is no use trying to deny it. Every organizer has to agitate in order to get people moving. But none dare expect thanks for it afterward.

The main agitator of the American revolution was Samuel Adams, whom history has relegated to a relatively minor role. In fact, the Revolution was, in his cousin John's words, "Sam's personal creation." It was Sam Adams who used incidents like the Stamp Act and the Tea Tax and even the overblown "Boston Massacre" to arouse his fellow countrymen to armed revolt.

The organizer is the person who asks the questions no one else is asking: "Why are things the way they are?" "Who made that decision?" "Why do you put up with this situation?" "What are you going to do about it?"

What makes these questions even more resented is that they are being asked by an outsider. The best organizers are "outsiders" for two reasons. First, only an outsider can come into a community without pre-conceived notions and loyalties. One cannot change what one does not recognize as changeable. Second, the process of agitating will cause enough ene-mies and scars that, when it is all over, it is best for the organizer to leave. That is easier to do if one was an outsider from the beginning.

Sam Adams died an outsider to the very government he had agitated into existence, buried in an unmarked grave.

The vocation of an organizer is to agitate—to "put things in motion"—and then to move on to another challenge. But the sowing of discontent is not—as the existing power struc-ture always suspects—around issues or forms of government or even distribution of money and power, although these always play a part. Rather, the agitation of people is primarily to get them to take control of their own lives, to demand the dignity and respect that is due them, to grow to the ultimate of their capabilities, and to build an organization that can last beyond themselves.

It is in this way that the organizer adopts the methods of St. Paul and Sam Adams.

THE ORGANIZER AS RADICAL

Likewise, organizers are accused of being radicals—which they are in much the same way that they are agitators. They are not radicals in the sense that they are communists or fas-cists or some kind of left or right wing ideologues. A good orga-nizer is neither because it interferes with the job. The organizer is not someone who has all the answers and then tries to convince people of them. The organizer's ideology is democracy—that people have the answers, if only they had the power to give them.

The question that divides democratic organizers from those who pose as organizers is: "Do people have the right to be wrong?"

This is the radical, the "root" concern, that precedes all others. Like the paternalistic missionary, it is very easy to de-cide that people are not "ready" for responsibility. Therefore, the organizer (or the politician or the bureaucrat or the Church official or the media) will make key decisions for them.

But what if people are stubborn? Or unreasonable? Or misinformed? Or cruel?

The organizer's answer is a leap of faith that people will be right more often than wrong, and certainly more often than those presently making decisions for them. If people are stubborn, unreasonable, misinformed or cruel, it is because they are motivated by fear and ignorance based on their life experience. Give them the power—and the responsibility for their actions—and they will begin making the "correct" decision most of the time. And when they do not, often they will prove themselves to have been right—albeit sometimes for the "wrong" reasons. For those times that they are dead wrong, it is the price that must be paid for democracy unless another, worse system is to be adopted.

This faith in people does not mean that the organizer has to organize for the Ku Klux Klan. Organizers bring their own values and self-interest to every situation and must not violate the basic tenets of religion and morality to which they subscribe.

But there is a wisdom in average, ordinary Americans which the true radical admires and wants to unleash.

The organizer is a radical not about ends—or solutions. Organizers are usually as surprised as anybody at what those turn out to be. The organizer is a radical about the means—how decisions are made and who makes them.

THE ORGANIZER AS REFLECTOR

The most curious discovery that the young organizer makes is that the most important part of the job is not action but reflection. The hardest skill to teach leaders is not how to act, but how to think.

The best reason to act is to have something to think about. The best reason for thinking is to direct our actions. Organizing is fertile ground for both. Ernest Dimnet points out in *The Art of Thinking* that ". . . action not only can help thought, but it produces it with a continuity which raises it to the height of creativeness."⁴⁷

It is only the mature organizer who can be helpful to leaders in learning this skill. For the first few years of a career, the organizer is too busy learning about action to bother about reflection. Only after there is relative security in the ability to cause things to happen can the organizer begin to think about what is actually happening. And only after organizers can reflect on what they are doing can they possibly help others to think.

Think about what? Think about meaning, and process, and results. Think about self-interest. Think about questions of morality and theology and philosophy. Think creatively about new ideas that haven't been tried or old ideas that need to be rethought and retried.

Think how? Systematically, disciplined, prayerfully. Think in writing. Think while reading. Think alone. Think with others.

If an organizer has a key one hour meeting with a leader, it might cost three additional hours of reflection: one beforehand, one afterward, and one in discussing it with a colleague or supervisor.

Where is that leader coming from, how has the leader's self-interest changed, what are the next steps in the leader's development, how can the organizer agitate the leader to get there? How prepared had the organizer been? How alert? What had gone right, what could have been done differently? Was the organizer's own self-interest being met by the relationship with the leader? Was it still enjoyable and challenging? How did the leader's development or lack of it affect the organization as a whole? What did it mean for other leaders, for issues in which the organization was presently involved, for that leader's congregation?

Then the organizer might review the strategic plan for the organization. What assumptions now need to be questioned, what adjustments made? Perhaps, for example, the leader had indicated—either directly or indirectly—that it was not in the leader's best interest to spend the time away from his or her family in order to be a candidate for one of the top leadership slots in the organization or the congregation. That one decision might change fifty different items on the organizer's agenda.

Finally, the organizer would reflect about what work that one meeting had generated. Who else now had to be talked to? What research facts had come to light that had to be checked out? What books or articles had to be read?

All of this should then be written down somewhere in cryptic notes so that it could be recalled—perhaps in the hour of thinking before the next meeting with that particular leader.

That kind of reflection is hard work, but it is nowhere near as difficult as teaching leaders how to do it. Yet this is the organizer's most important legacy.

THE ORGANIZER AS STRATEGIC PLANNER

American congregations do little or no strategic planning. If there is any one reason that they are losing the value war to the forces of materialism, this is it.

The dean of American management consultants, Peter Drucker, in his classic work *Management* argues persuasively for the absolute necessity of every organization—profit making or not—to do strategic planning:

> Management has no choice but to anticipate the future, to attempt to mold it, and to balance short-range and long-range goals. It is not given to mortals to do well any of these things. But lacking divine guidance, management must make sure that these difficult responsibilities are not overlooked or neglected but taken care of as well as is humanly possible.

The future will not just happen if one wishes hard enough. It requires decision—now. It imposes risks—now. It requires action—now. It demands allocation of resources, and, above all, of human resources—now. It requires work—now.[48]

The organizer is uniquely positioned to teach this skill to the leaders of congregations because it is an absolutely essential exercise for the success of the community organization effort and therefore provides an arena for leaders to test the concept. The community organization ultimately has very little inherent power and must rely on its wits and guts to win. One of the ways to do that is with systematic strategic planning that positions the organization in the right place at the right time to be effective.

For example, the Queens Citizens Organization adopted as its first county-wide issue a campaign against arson in the borough—not because arson was the most immediate concern of residents but because the leaders of the organization could look across their own borders to Brooklyn and the Bronx and realize that if they did not act now they would face the same fate that afflicted those parts of New York City.

Likewise, the congregation that does not look regularly at its demographic projections, at its finances, at its physical plant, at its allocation of resources, at its mix of programs, at its liturgy, at its educational efforts, is doomed to the same extinction that has occurred in many once-vibrant churches and synagogues. Leaders from the Queens organization were able to go back to their own congregations and apply the same principles of strategic planning that they had used on community issues.

As simple a question as the succession of leadership is often ignored by most congregations. Does a major corporation know who its next chief executive officer will be? Certainly. Does it know who the one after that will be? Probably, and if it doesn't then you can bet that there are either two candidates being tested and trained or a massive talent search is underway. Does the average American congregation know who its next president will be even a month before the election or appointment?

A good organizer must be a good strategic planner and a good strategic planning teacher. Leaders of the organization must be taught how to assess their present program, how to adopt goals, how to set immediate objectives, how to organize to achieve those objectives and how to constantly re-evaluate their execution of those plans—both for the community organization and for the member congregations.

THE ORGANIZER AS TACTICIAN

Community organization is an adversarial process. There is no way to sugar-coat that truth. Organizing people who do not have power will always cause those who have it to fight to keep it. People are never given power; they must demand it and take it. Therefore, organizers must be fighters if they are going to be useful to the people for whom they work.

During the "Save-the-Cities Campaign" for more mortgage money in the Twin Cities, the organizers suggested that the organization tactically keep negotiating simultaneously with the two major savings and loan associations in Minnesota: Twin Cities Federal and Midwest Federal. Both institutions happened to hold their annual meetings on the same day in Minneapolis. The organization announced that it would show up at one of the meetings to sign an agreement, but refused to say which. Several hundred people rallied at a church halfway between the two banks to vote on whose offer to accept. Both banks, of course, had to prepare for huge crowds, putting extra pressure on them during the negotiations and giving the media a classic story of citizen power.

This kind of social jujitsu is the only way that community organizations can ever beat opponents bigger than themselves. Organizers must know both how to think tactically themselves and how to teach leaders to do the same.

THE ORGANIZER AS LEADER

There are times when the organizer must function as a leader. This is the hardest role for the organizer to keep straight because it seems to contradict the work of training and developing others.

In the beginning of any organizing drive, there are no real leaders around. In fact, the organizer is often the only one with a real vision of what the organization is all about and at that stage often wants it to succeed more than anyone else. So the organizer becomes *de facto* the leader of the organization. But that situation has to change very soon if the organization is to have a chance of success, and even then the hard feelings caused by this appropriation of the legitimate role of the leader is one of the main reasons why the organizer should and must leave the organization after two or three years.

Even after the organization has matured, there are instances when the organizer has to assume a leadership role—either to show leaders how to do something, or to prove that the organizer can and will do what is being asked of the leaders, or because the situation is so new and so critical that the organizer's skills and experience are vital to success.

Sometimes organizers have to lead out of their own need. Most often this is because they are still learning themselves. When I first tried to teach people how to raise money, I had to lead a lot of appeals myself in order to understand how the leaders were feeling when asking for money. Only after I had that experience could I teach others how to do it. There was no other way for me to learn.

Other times, organizers must lead an action just to get their own juices flowing again, to remember why they are doing what they are doing, to feel the anger and frustration that the leaders feel.

There are two kinds of organizers to avoid: those who want to lead too much and those who will never lead. The former will dominate the organization and stifle the leaders; the latter will let the leaders drown and the organization flounder.

THE ORGANIZER AS PROFESSIONAL

There are a lot of young people—and even a very few older ones—who are organizers because organizing is a cause, because it fulfills their ideology. They are therefore able to work for very low wages and under miserable conditions because they are being paid in other ways. In truth, these people are subsidizing the organizations that they work for with time and commitment, if not money.

For several reasons, I do not believe that these are the best organizers for a serious community organization to consider hiring.

1. Enthusiastic is not necessarily competent. Many organizations pay the price of being the training grounds for would-be organizers, and I confess that several have paid that price in my career. The fact that the organizer is cheap is an extremely short-term view of the organization's investment and worth.

2. It is hard to hold low-paid organizers accountable. The threat of losing their job is not very real if they are making less than a clerk in a local grocery store.

3. Because their salaries are so low, there is little need for the organizers to put the organization on a strong financial footing. Then, if they should leave the organization, it is in no position to hire a replacement—unless it can find another dedicated person to work for next to nothing.

4. It is very difficult for an organizer to develop the personal and family stability needed to do the job well if there is constant worry about personal finances. Organizers who are poor are like all other poor people: they are distracted about material things. There is also a simple matter of justice. An organization that is paying poverty wages to its own staff will have a difficult time fighting for justice for its members.

5. If they are in fact subsidizing the organization with their labor, then the organizers will expect and demand a decision-making role in the organization whether that is in the interest of the organization or not. It will be their issues, their ideologies, their agendas that will predominate in the organization.

A professional organizer with the ability to agitate, to teach, to reflect, to do strategic planning, to fight, to lead is a rare commodity. To keep one, an organization should be prepared to pay a professional compensation, including salary, pension, benefits and expenses.

Organizing then becomes a new career possibility that parents and clergy can hold out to promising young people as something with a future for basically stable, family-oriented individuals. It then takes an honored place among recognized vocations for laypeople.

In his paper, *Making an Offer We Can't Refuse,* Richard Harmon summed up the role of the professional organizer:

> Organizing is teaching.
>
> Obviously, not academic-type teaching, which is confined for the most part to stuffing data into people's ears. Organizing is teaching which rests on people's life experiences, drawing them out, developing trust, going into action, disrupting old perceptions of reality, developing group solidarity, watching the growth of confidence to continue to act, then sharing in the emotional foundation for continual questioning of the then-current status quo.[49]

ONE ORGANIZER

One of the best fictional depictions of an organizer is in Ken Kesey's famous novel turned into an award winning movie, *One Flew Over the Cuckoo's Nest.*

McMurphy is an organizer, and the ward in the insane asylym is a metaphor for our society. McMurphy dies in the end, but remember that his protégé, Chief Broom, escapes from his self-imposed isolation to return home and become a leader of his people.

Nurse Ratched is the existing power structure, and she recognizes that the organizer is a threat to the way things are.

To her, McMurphy is a manipulator. To the residents of the asylum, he is a savior . . . a missionary.

> "What, Miss Ratched, is your opinion of this new patient? I mean, gee, he's good-looking and friendly and everything, but in my humble opinion he certainly takes *over*."
>
> The Big Nurse tests a needle against her fingertip. "I'm afraid"—she stabs the needle down in the rubber-capped vial and lifts the plunger—"that is exactly what the new patient is planning: to take over. He is what we call a 'manipulator,' Miss Flinn, a man who will use everyone and everything to his own ends."
>
> "Oh, but. I mean, in a mental hospital? What could his ends be?"
>
> "Any number of things." She's calm, smiling, lost in the work of loading the needles. "Comfort and an easy life, for instance; the feeling of power and respect, perhaps; monetary gain—perhaps all of these things. Sometimes a manipulator's own ends are simply the actual *disruption* of the ward for the sake of disruption. There are such people in our society. A manipulator can influence the other patients and disrupt them to such an extent that it may take months to get everything running smooth once more. With the present permissive philosophy in mental hospitals, it's easy for them to get away with it. Some years back it was quite different. I recall some years back we had a man, a Mr. Taber, on the ward, and he was an *intolerable* Ward Manipulator. For a while." She looks up from her work, needle half filled in front of her face like a little wand. Her eyes get far-off and pleased with the memory.
>
> "But, gee," the other nurse says, "what on earth would *make* a man want to do something like disrupt the ward for, Miss Ratched? What possible motive . . . ?"[50]

NOTES

1. Peter Berger and Richard Neuhaus, *To Empower People: The Role of Mediating Structures in Public Policy* (Washington: American Enterprise Institute, 1977), p. 2.

2. Mary John Manazan, ed., in Carlos Abesamis, *Salvation: Historical and Total*, introduction, as quoted in Arthur Jones, "Bishops' Collegiality—So Far, So Good," *National Catholic Reporter*, February 4, 1983, p. 24.

3. Walter Rauschenbusch, *Righteousness of the Kingdom*, ed. Max Stackhouse (Nashville: Abingdon Press, 1968), pp. 189–190.

4. Paul Moore, Jr., "Koch, Reagan and the Poor," *The New York Times*, January 31, 1982, p. E 21.

5. Morris Adler, "Torah and Society," in *Great Jewish Ideas* as printed in Norbert Brockman, S.M. and Nicholas Piediscalzi, eds., *Religion and Social Responsibility* (New York: Alba House, 1973), p. 13.

6. Peter Berger, *The Noise of the Solemn Assemblies* (Garden City: Doubleday and Company, 1961), p. 178.

7. Paul VI, *Octogesima Adveniens* in David O'Brien and Thomas Shannon, eds., *Renewing the Earth* (Garden City: Doubleday and Company, 1977), p. 380.

8. Andrew Greeley, "People and Values," column, 1981. Used with permission.

9. Ignazio Silone, *Bread and Wine* (New York: Harper and Brothers, 1937), pp. 135–138. Used with permission.

10. Stephen Bouman, *Toward Politically Informed Love*, unpublished doctoral dissertation, New York Theological Seminary, 1980.

11. Ivan Illich, *The Church, Change and Development* (Chicago: Urban Training Center Press/Herder and Herder, 1970), p. 44.

12. Harvey Seifert, *New Power for the Church* (Philadelphia: The Westminster Press, 1976), pp. 139–140.

13. John Coleman, *An American Strategic Theology* (New York/Ramsey: Paulist Press, 1982), pp. 269–270.

14. Richard Johnson, *Reflections on Self-Interest and Power: A Theological Justification for Community Organization* (St. Paul: Twin Cities Organization), p. 3.

15. Jacques Maritain, *Reflections on America* (New York: Gordian Press, 1975), p. 162.

16. Lester Thurow, *The Zero Sum Society* (New York: Basic Books, 1980), p. 24.

17. Emil Fackenheim, "A Jewish View of Religious Responsibility for the Social Order," in Earl Raab, ed., *Religious Conflict in America* (New York: Anchor Books, 1964), pp. 134–135.

18. Richard Johnson, *loc. cit.*

19. Louis Raths, Merrill Harmin, and Sidney Simon, *Values and Teaching*, 2nd ed. (Columbus: Charles E. Merrill Publishing Company, 1966), p. 28.

20. Christopher Lasch, *The Culture of Narcissism* (New York: W.W. Norton and Company, 1978); see also *Haven in a Heartless World* (New York: Basic Books, 1977).

21. Industrial Areas Foundation, *Organizing for Family and Congregation* (Huntington: Industrial Areas Foundation, 1978), pp. 3–4.

22. David O'Brien, "Some Reflections on the Catholic Experience in the United States," in Irene Woodward, ed., *Catholic Church: United States Experience* (New York/Ramsey: Paulist Press, 1979), p. 33.

23. *Ibid*, p. 29.

24. Anne Marie Hauck Walsh, *The Public's Business: The Politics and Practices of Government Corporations* (Cambridge: MIT Press, 1980), pp. 12–13.

25. J. Phillip Wogamon, "The Church as Mediating Institution: Theological and Philosophical Perspective," in Michael Novak, ed., *Democracy and Mediating Structures: A Theological Inquiry* (Washington: American Enterprise Institute, 1980) p. 77.

26. John Hermann Randall, Jr., "The Importance of Being Unprincipled," in *The American Scholar*, April 1938, pp. 131–143.

27. David H. Benke, "Practical Ecumenism: 'Rebuilding the Walls,'" *Lutheran Forum*, Pentecost 1983, p. 11.

28. Reinhold Niebuhr, *Moral Man and Immoral Society*, rev. ed. (New York: Charles Scribner's Sons, 1960), p. 172.

29. Evelyn and James Whitehead, *Community of Faith: Models and Strategies for Building Christian Communities* (New York: The Seabury Press, 1982), pp. 126–127.

30. Reinhold Niebuhr, *op. cit.*, p. 22.

31. Nick Salvatore, *Eugene V. Debs: Citizen and Socialist*, The Working Class in American History (Urbana/Chicago/London: University of Illinois Press, 1982), pp. 262–302.

32. Kenneth Bacon, "Rumors of Stockman's Departure Persist As Other Reagan Aides Rise in Influence," *The Wall Street Journal*, September 15, 1982, p. 50.

33. Anne Keegan, "Father Hit Cult Where It Hurt—Pocketbook," *Chicago Tribune*, March 26, 1982, p. 20. Used with permission.

34. Richard Hirsch, *Judaism and Cities in Crisis*, excerpted as "The Jew and the City," in Brockman and Piediscalzi, eds., *op. cit.*, p. 311

35. Administrative Board of the the United States Catholic Conference, *Political Responsibility: Reflections on an Election Year*, in O'Brien and Shannon, eds., *op. cit.*, p. 529.

36. John Egan, *Remarks of Msgr. John J. Egan* (Chicago: The Midwest Academy, 1976)

37. William Droel, "Confident Laity," *The Other Side*, June 1982, p. 32.

38. Nicholas Von Hoffman, "Finding and Making Leaders," publishing information unavailable. Used with permission.

39. *Ibid.*

40. *Ibid.*

41. Juan Luis Segundo, *A Theology for Artisans of a New Humanity: The Community Called Church*, Vol. 1 (Maryknoll: Orbis Press, 1973), p. 81.

42. Douglas Hyde, *Dedication and Leadership* (Notre Dame: University of Notre Dame Press, 1966) p. 27.

43. David O'Brien, *op. cit.*, p. 34.

44. James Luther Adams, *On Being Human Religiously* (Boston: Beacon Press, 1978), p. 59.

45. Henri Nouwen, *Creative Ministry* (New York: Doubleday and Company, 1971), p. 74.

46. Roland Allen, *Missionary Methods: St. Paul's or Ours?* (Grand Rapids: William B. Eerdmans Publishing Company, 1962), epilogue.

47. Ernest Dimnet, *The Art of Thinking* (New York: Fawcett Premier, 1956), p. 77.

48. Peter Drucker, *Management* (New York: Harper and Row, 1973), pp. 121–122.

49. Richard Harmon, *Making an Offer We Can't Refuse* (Huntington: Industrial Areas Foundation, 1973), p. 1.

50. Ken Kesey, *One Flew Over the Cuckoo's Nest* (New York: New American Library, 1962), pp. 29–30. Used with permission.

INDEX